GOLF'S MOST ASTONISHING ROUND

GOLF'S MOST ASTONISHING ROUND

The Story of Ernie Foord, Somerset's Unsung Genius of Golf

Anthony Gibson

Foreword by Tony Hill
Former President of the English Golf Union

CHARLCOMBE BOOKS

Text © Anthony Gibson

Charlcombe Books
125 Garnet Street, Bristol BS3 3JH
tel: 01174 523760

First published 2023

ISBN: 978 1 7399293 3 6

Printed and bound in Great Britain by
CPI Antony Rowe, Bumpers Farm, Chippenham SN14 6LH

Contents

	Foreword by Tony Hill	7
	Acknowledgements	8
	Introduction	9
1	In the beginning	12
2	'A world's record'	36
3	Ernie in The Open	53
4	A professional's life	62
5	That most remarkable round of golf	71
6	Last years at Burnham	89
7	Ernie (and Fred) in America	94
8	Oakland Hills	99
9	In conclusion	107
	Index	111
	Books by Anthony Gibson	112

Tony Hill

Foreword by Tony Hill

From my earliest days as a junior member of Burnham and Berrow Golf Club I was made well aware of the history and traditions of the club. A number of the more senior members were happy to pass on their memories of the development of the course and of some of the great characters of the past. Included among these were Sammy Woods, the outstanding Australia, England and Somerset cricketer and international rugby player, Sydney Fry, who was many times English amateur champion at both billiards and snooker as well as being an international golfer, Ben Travers, distinguished playwright and fanatical supporter of English cricket, and Jack Lysaght, an all-round sportsman who was wont to enter the bar with his pet monkey on his shoulder.

It was on hearing that Sammy Woods had taken part in a cross-country match from the first tee at Weston-super-Mare to the 18th hole at Burnham that four members of the Leatherjackets Golfing Society, including myself, decided to re-enact this encounter some 60 years later in 1968.

But the character and charm of the club that still exists today was formed not only by the members but also by the secretaries, stewards, greenkeepers and in particular the professionals who all left their mark in one way or another over the years.

The village of Berrow produced an extraordinary number of golf professionals and, of these, Burnham was fortunate to have the services of two Foords, father Walter and son Ernie, and three Bradbeers, to follow on from the legendary JH Taylor. It is the career of Ernie Foord and his barely believable round of 73, played entirely with a putter, that is at the heart of this engaging and diligently researched book in which Anthony Gibson gives us a splendid feel of the golf and golfers of the early 20th century.

Tony Hill has been a member of Burnham and Berrow Golf Club since 1952, was the Club's President from 2009 to 2013 and was President of the English Golf Union, now England Golf, in 1990.

Acknowledgements

My thanks go to Tony Hill for checking the accuracy of my account of Burnham and Berrow GC's early history, to Jay Hults and Martin Schemm of Plum Hollow, to David Baugham and Richard Howting of Oakland Hills, to Maggie Lagle of the USGA and, most of all, to David Haines for his photographic skills, his guidance on the early layout of the course and for his enthusiasm for the entire project. As a local boy, a brilliant golfer, custodian of Burnham and Berrow's history, and the club's greatly respected current Professional, he is in the true tradition of JH Taylor, the Bradbeers and, of course, Ernie Foord.

And, of course, my most sincere thanks to my wonderfully patient and eagle-eyed publisher Stephen Chalke.

Introduction

This is the story of a golfer of whom very few people, even at his home club of Burnham and Berrow in Somerset, have heard. Yet Ernie Foord was a remarkable golfer and a remarkable man. The eldest boy in a family of seven, born in humble circumstances in the village of Berrow, he graduated from scruffy caddy to club professional at the age of 16 and set what was regarded at the time as a world-record low score, before emigrating to the USA during the First World War, eventually becoming the professional at the US Open venue of Oakland Hills, ahead of all the star American pros of his day. All that, and then there is the inspiration for this account of his life: he once went round Burnham and Berrow's notoriously difficult championship course in 73 strokes, using just his putter.

Ernie competed in the Open Championship on eleven occasions, without ever doing himself justice. His real strength was as a match player. In 1913 he took on his mentor, five-time Open Champion JH Taylor over 36 holes at Burnham and beat him. In 1920 he and his younger brother Fred got the better of six-time Open winner Harry Vardon and Ted Ray, fresh from taking the US Open, in a 36-hole challenge match. A year later, it was the turn of the reigning Open and US Open champions, Jock Hutchinson and Jim Barnes, to be served humble pie by the Ford brothers, as they had by then become.

We know the bare bones of Ernie Foord's life. Putting flesh on them has been another matter. Burnham and Berrow has excellent records, lovingly preserved by the current professional, David Haines. But golf club committees in the Edwardian age weren't really too concerned about the deeds of their professionals on the course. If the tee boxes had sand in them, the flags in the greens were in the right spots, the members could get their clubs mended well and swiftly and lessons were provided as required, then that was really the extent of their interest in their club professional, club servant as he was. So Ernie's course record 63 – the equivalent of a 58 or 59 on today's course – merits not a mention in the committee minutes. His 73 with a putter – the subject of a Bernard Darwin column in *The Times* – is ignored. And perhaps most sadly of all, the letter he was sent before he emigrated, expressing the club's appreciation for his services, was not included in the minutes and has not, as far as we know, survived.

'As far as we know'. That proviso appears all too frequently in the account that follows. We do have detailed accounts of Ernie's matches against JH Taylor at Burnham, and *Golf Illustrated* did provide the hole-by-hole scores for his course record of 63. But for most of his other feats, including his 73 with his putter, even the scorecards have not survived. So I have had to employ a certain amount of poetic licence when it comes to the details, although the accounts are, I believe, true to the B&B club and course as it was at the time, and to the qualities of Ernie Foord as a man and a golfer.

Researching Ernie's career in the USA has been even more frustrating, not helped by the fact that the clubhouses of the final three golf clubs at which he was professional during the 20s and 30s have all been burned down, their archives mostly destroyed. But, with the help of kind members of the Plum Hollow and Oakland Hills golf clubs and of the USGA's Librarian Maggie Lagle, I have been able to piece together at least the highlights of his time in Kansas City and Michigan.

It is a particular shame that so few photographs of Ernie Foord have survived. That of him driving at the old eighth in his 1901 match with JH Taylor gives a good idea of the sort of golfer he was: not tall, lightly built, but strong and wiry, with a powerful, cut-off swing, perfect for drilling the ball through the Burnham winds. In those broad, rustic features and generous smile as the US Open presentation is made at Oakland Hills in 1924, you can see the man of Somerset.

The little village of Berrow has produced a quite remarkable number of professional golfers down the years. We think immediately of the Whitcombes, Ernest, Charles and Reg, Ryder Cuppers all, and Reg the Open Champion in 1938. Or the seven Bradbeer brothers who became successful, tournament-winning pros, Bob, his brother Fred and son Richard serving Burnham for a combined total of 60 years. Ernie Foord and his brother Fred may be less well-known than those champions, but their names may stand proudly alongside them in any roll-call of golfing achievement.

If this account of Ernie Foord's life and achievements, incomplete as it is, can help to bring him out of the shadows of golfing history and into the light, then that is surely no less than he deserves.

A factual detail

Keen students of the history of Burnham and Berrow Golf Club may notice that I have written of a match in April 1901 between JH Taylor and Ernie Foord, played to celebrate the opening of the extended course. In 'Between the Church and the Lighthouse', Philip Richards' well-researched history of the club, this match is said to have taken place in 1907. The misunderstanding has occurred as a result of ambiguous handwriting in the carefully preserved scrapbooks of the club's early history.

Any possible doubt is removed by the report that is cut out of the Western Counties Graphic. It refers to JH Taylor as 'the present Open Golf Champion', which he was in April 1901 but not in April 1907.

1

In the beginning

The village of Berrow was a rather scruffy, down at heel, out of the way sort of place in the second half of the nineteenth century. Straggling along the road from Burnham-on-Sea to Brean, it was notable mainly for the towering sand dunes, known locally as the 'sand-tots', which separated it from the sea and which, when a storm roared in from Bridgwater Bay, would threaten to engulf its handsome 13th century church, if not the village itself.

The duneland was owned by the Lords of the Manor, Peregrine Francis and Peregrine Hammond of Berrow Manor. They used it, Hammond mostly, as a rabbit warren, while what little grazing there was in the hollows between the sand mountains was let to local farmers and small-holders for pasturing their sheep, cattle and horses, and the villagers also enjoyed limited rights to take rabbits for the pot and sand for their gardens. It was not a wealthy community. There were still one or two fishermen, setting their nets to catch salmon and sea trout along Gore sands, but most of the men worked on the local farms. The late eighteen-hundreds was a time of agricultural depression, brought on by a malevolent combination of a series of poor harvests at home and an influx of cheap grain and refrigerated meat from abroad. The dairymen on Metford Frost's farm on the Brean road were probably taking home 15 shillings a week, but an ordinary farm labourer, or one of Mr Hammond's warreners, would be lucky to get ten shillings a week, the equivalent of just £60 in today's money. With only the most rudimentary forms of birth control available, families were large, money was short and food was precious. Many of the parents of the eighty or so girls and boys at Berrow Village School couldn't afford the cost of educating their children, especially when it doubled from a penny a week to twopence in 1887, and truancy rates were high. Berrow was a village badly in need of a shot in the arm.

It came, quite by chance, in 1890. One evening that summer, the Reverend Canon Hegan Kennard, a distinguished Catholic priest and well-connected golfer at Westward Ho! *, was walking back from Brean to catch a train at Burnham and decided to take a short cut through the Berrow sandhills. Then, as now, a sandy track ran from the church and manor house along the eastern edge of the dunes to the outskirts of the town. It was a fine evening, and Canon Kennard, as he was always known, who had never come this way before, decided to climb the nearest ridge of sandhills to get a proper look at his surroundings.

"My goodness," he gasped to himself, as he looked out across a mountain range of dunes towards the sea and the setting sun, the Quantocks purple in the distance. "If ever there was a place that the Almighty intended for a golf course, then this is surely it. Sandhills to drive over, bunkers for hazards, hollows for greens and what turf there is looks beautifully firm and crisp." He looked up to the heavens and brought his hands together in a gesture of prayer: "Thank you, Lord, for guiding my footsteps to this place. With your strength and my will, we shall make this the finest golf course in all England."

It was indeed a most fortunate revelation. Golf was just beginning to catch on in England at the time. All over the country, bands of golfing enthusiasts were casting hopeful and ambitious eyes on stretches of linksland, moor, heather and heath. And Canon Kennard's was an educated eye. He already knew more than enough about the game to understand that if the right stretch of country was one pre-requisite for a successful new venture, then an ample supply of keen and determined local supporters was a second, a sufficiency of funds a third, and a respected course designer a fourth.

He wasted no time. First he contacted his friends Tom and William Holt, who owned the local brewery, Holt Brothers of Burnham, and whom he knew were anxious to take up this newly fashionable game. Between them they put together an invitation list of local dignitaries, retired army officers prominent amongst them, and invited them to a

---

His brother, Col Edmond Hegan Kennard, was at various times captain of Royal North Devon, Blackheath, Wimbledon and Hoylake, which can't have left him much time for his duties as an MP!

meeting at what was then one of Somerset's smartest hotels, the Royal Clarence at Bridgwater. Glasses charged, pipes lit, seats taken, Canon Kennard addressed the meeting:

"Gentlemen," he began, for there were certainly no ladies present! "We have been blessed – and I use the word advisedly – in this part of Somerset by having on our very doorstep what is potentially one of the finest stretches of golfing country in the entire kingdom. Golf offers diverting exercise in God's fresh air, it will bring visitors flocking to your town, it will provide much needed employment as caddies or on the course for the local men and boys, and I already know from my contacts with Mr Hammond that the land which we need on Berrow Warren may well be available, subject of course to goodwill on both sides.

"I hereby propose that we form a Burnham-on-Sea golf club, setting up a committee to bring it into being and manage it thereafter. It will be the West Country's golfing jewel and a boon and blessing to our town." The eleven other gentlemen present clapped, hear-heared or banged the tables in agreement and support.

The enthusiasm wasn't quite universal. One man, a well-to-do farmer and landowner, did warn that, on the basis of experience at Westward Ho!, the Berrow villagers might not take kindly to being deprived of some of their grazing, sand-digging and rabbit-catching. But the counter-argument that any loss in that respect would be far outweighed by the jobs and money that a prestigious golf club would bring to the area carried the day.

"Think of it this way," announced Tom Holt. "If the Berrow men have a few more pennies in their pockets to spend on my excellent beer, they'll be far happier than scrabbling about in the sand trying to catch a few scrawny conies!"

So the motion was carried, unanimously. The club was formed, with Kennard as President, William Holt as Vice-President and Tom Holt as one of the joint secretaries. Kennard knew immediately who he would ask to lay out the new course – Royal North Devon's young Scottish professional, Charles Gibson, who had already made a significant mark in helping to re-model the course on Northam Burrows.

Monsignor Canon Kennard

Gibson made his first visit to Burnham in September. He maybe wasn't quite as effusive as Kennard – "it 'ud be a grand country if there wasnae quite sae much sand" were his initial thoughts – but he set to work with a will and by the turn of the year the new course – nine holes, roughly 2,400 yards, bogey 38 – had been designed and roughly laid out. Cowlin's Cottage, on the eastern edge of the dunes, at the end of a rough track leading up from the main Burnham road, close to the intended site for the club-house, was purchased to serve as accommodation for the steward, with a lean-to for the professional.

There was no shortage of local men to do the work involved in turfing, seeding, shifting sand, clearing the scrub and planting marram grass to try to stabilise the dunes. Local knowledge identified Walter Foord as the likeliest foreman for the job. He had just turned 30 and lived with his wife Sarah and family, just down the road at South Cottage. Walter was strong, in mind as well as body, and he was ambitious for himself and his family. He worked hard and stood no nonsense, either from his fellow workers or from those who might consider themselves his betters. Walter Foord might have been content to describe himself as merely a 'labourer' when it came to completing the 1891 census form, but he was a man who commanded respect. He and Gibson got on well, especially after the Scotsman had thrust a club into Walter's hands, encouraged him "to gie the ba' a guid whack" and discovered that he had a natural golfing talent as his right-hand man.

The Foords were a happy family, for all that money had always been tight. Sarah came from the village of Shapwick on the Somerset peat moors, some ten miles south-east of Berrow, where she had been at school with the Whitcombe brothers, one of whom, Arthur, had recently come to work on the warren for Mr Hammond and who, with his wife Bessie, would produce one of the greatest golfing dynasties of them all. Sarah and Walter had married when they were just 20 and already had three fine boys: William, who was 10, Ernest 7 and little Fred, just 3. When Walter heard about the plans for a golf course, he could immediately sense the possibilities for himself and his boys. A golf course would bring money and jobs to 'Berrow-super-Rabbit-Burrows',

Staff preparing the course, 1891

A view of the club in its early days

as the village had derisively been dubbed by a visiting journalist; even shovelling sand and carrying clubs had to be more rewarding than mucking out pigsties or trying to catch rabbits.

Burnham Golf Club was fortunate indeed in its moving spirits and its early personnel. Canon Kennard's country-wide network of golfing contacts helped ensure that word of the new course was soon spread far and wide where it mattered most. The likes of Colonel Eliot Armstrong and William Akerman worked tirelessly to overcome local difficulties. The Holt family put up much of the capital that was needed, Tom Holt financing the £184 – 8s cost of a smart pavilion. Walter Foord soon proved himself to be as talented at green-keeping as he was as a course constructor.

And the first professional? Well, he was a certain John Henry Taylor, a young green-keeper at Westward Ho!, whom Kennard had seen defeat the great Horace Hutchinson, head to head, just two years previously. He may have been only 19 at the time, but both Kennard and Charles Gibson knew golfing talent when they saw it. Taylor would think long and hard before accepting their offer – it would mean leaving home, his mother and a safe job and committing himself to what was still very much an unknown quantity, but eventually "with £1 in my pocket borrowed from someone or somewhere, by my mother, a big wooden box, securely corded, containing my scanty wardrobe, I left on January 1st 1891, the home that had shielded and nurtured me for nineteen years, to face a new world that had yet to be explored."

Taylor needn't have worried. The new golf club got off to a flying start. By June of 1891, barely nine months since Kennard's fateful shortcut along the dunes, the course was ready and the 'pavilion' built. The official opening took place on June 4th, marked by a medal competition for the members in the morning and a match between JH Taylor and Horace Hutchinson in the afternoon, won by Taylor 2/1, so repeating his triumph of two years earlier – and this time he could afford to have more than one iron club in his bag!

Sadly, we don't know who the caddies were in that encounter, but it would be surprising if either Bill or Ernie Foord didn't feature, given that, thanks to their father's role, they must have known more about

JH Taylor, circa 1895

and putting in 1908

both the game of golf and the challenges posed by the new course, than any of their contemporaries. But for any boy over the age of about seven in Berrow – and there were probably 40 or 50 of them – the new course was a godsend, offering work, money (6d a round, no less), comradeship and, amongst themselves when no-one was looking, a great deal of rascally fun.

Caddying was hard work, of course. Most of the more regular Burnham golfers had their own caddies, who would be expected to clean and oil their clubs, dubbin their boots, collect their practice balls and turn up promptly on the first tee at starting time, there to produce a perfect little pyramid of sand on which his master's ball would be tee-ed. Those who didn't have a regular bag would gather outside the pro shop, marshalled by a caddy master, who would do the allocation of caddy to golfer and for whom the task must have been rather harder than it sounds, judging by the number of caddy-masters who came and went in the club's early years – at least two of them making off with the takings and never being seen again. However, in JH Taylor, the Berrow caddies had their champion and their mentor.

It was, after all, only a few years since he'd been a caddy himself and no little angel either, judging by the account in *Golf: My Life's Work*:

> I made a little niche for myself among the other hooligans, and, had I not known of them before, would have been initiated into various dodges, tricks and evasions which the gang employed. For instance, if we saw a golfer coming who was disliked or who had the reputation of being harsh or stingy, away the whole lot would skedaddle, in hiding until the player was seen leaving the first tee, forced to carry his own clubs as a punishment. Believe me – and later experiences have proved its accuracy – the young caddie is a most discerning creature. He will respond readily to kind and humane treatment and give of his best in return, but once his susceptibilities are aroused, the player may expect, if not open hostility, a grudging and unsatisfactory service. The caddie has a way of getting his own back.

Hooligans and discerning creatures the Berrow caddies may or may not have been, but what was remarkable about them was their aptitude for the game. They took to it with a vengeance. A few lucky ones would manage to get hold of an ancient club or two and a handful of battered gutties. Those less fortunate resorted to making their own clubs, from a roughly hewn chunk of wood, a stout ash wand rammed through a hole in it as a shaft. As for balls, one of the caddie's most important duties was to spot and then to find his master's ball, after a wild or mishit shot. Failure to do so could, with some of the more irascible Burnham golfers, lead to pennies being docked from the fee. But the really cunning caddies, with a more benevolent master, when sent off alone into a particularly wild piece of country, would pretend that their search had been in vain, whereas in reality they had found the ball and concealed it in a convenient rabbit burrow – of which there were many – for recovery later under cover of darkness.

So when the Berrow caddies weren't at school, which seems to have been most of the time, or carrying clubs, they would be practising their golfing skills on the huge area of burrows to the north of the course proper. It was rough country, and the equipment was as precious as it was rudimentary, which together put a huge premium on hitting the ball where you intended it to go. Sometimes they would dig a rough hole in one of the flatter areas and practice chipping and putting. Or they might set a mark hundreds of yards away and play a sort of long-distance, cross-country golf, each caddy going on ahead after playing his shot, so as to spot the efforts of his companions. They weren't coached, of course. JH Taylor's services in that regard were reserved strictly for the members and their guests. But they had every opportunity to watch and to learn, and what better model could any young aspiring golfer have than the swing of JH Taylor, especially on a windswept links like Burnham?

'JH had not the rhythmic grace of Vardon, nor the 'divine fury' of Braid,' wrote Bernard Darwin*. 'But that flat-footed hit with the little

---

* *'Life is Sweet Brother' by Bernard Darwin. Darwin, grandson of the naturalist Charles Darwin, wrote on golf for* The Times *from 1907 to 1953; he was the first man to cover the game on a regular basis,* grunt and the arms tucked into the left-side gave me a more ecstatic sensation than either. He was, in a way, too, the most exciting, just because he seemed to be playing, as near as might be, the same stroke all the time.'

No wonder that so many of the Berrow caddies who saw JH Taylor play at close quarters would go on to become professional golfers of the highest calibre themselves.

And of the earliest generation of Berrow caddies, Ernie Foord was unquestionably the best golfer. Even when he was only eight years old, there seemed to be nothing he couldn't do with a golf ball. In much the same way as Severiano Ballesteros would later learn to play every shot in the book by practising with a 3-iron, Ernie honed his skills using an ancient cut-down cleek. The fact that his parents were by now living in Golf Cottage, behind the clubhouse – his mother Sarah as caretaker, his father Walter as head green-keeper – was a particular blessing. Whenever the opportunity presented itself, usually in the half-light after the last of the gentlemen golfers had left for home, the three Foord boys could slip out onto the links, their mother and father turning a diplomatic blind eye, to practise their skills.

Ernie became quite remarkably proficient with his single club. Watching Taylor, plus a kindly word here and there, had shown him how vital it was to be able to shape and manoeuvre the ball when the wind was blowing (which at Burnham was virtually all the time). By opening the face and keeping the weight on his right side, he could hit his cleek as high as a mashie shot. Taylor's example had taught him the draw, the fade and, crucially, the push-shot – played by hitting hard down on the ball, positioned right back in the stance, so as to drill it unfeasible distances through even the strongest of the Burnham winds. Two principles which JH dinned into him he never forgot: "There are no hazards in the air" and "What's the matter with the middle of the course?"

He could putt as well; my, could he putt! Not even Taylor himself was more adept at picking the right line on the contoured, sandy greens, and when it came to striking the ball up to the hole Ernie was quite fearless – as indeed were all the young caddies, their nerves as yet unscarred by painful golfing experience. If they struck it six feet past, well, so what? They would always hole the one back, and what was the point in leaving any putt short? "Never up, never in, sir": wasn't that what Canon Kennard was so fond of saying, as yet another of his partner's putts pulled up six inches short?

JH Taylor wasn't at Burnham very long. He was happy enough there and would often say in later years how much he had learned about iron play from playing to the small Burnham greens in the relentless Burnham winds, but his duties as professional included helping Walter Foord keep the course in good order, and that was a lot more difficult than it sounds. The course's previous use as a warren meant that there were rabbits everywhere. Worms were another constant menace – "every night, every green was covered in their casts which had to be swept away in the morning," lamented Heneage Wheeler, the grandson of a vicar of Berrow, who wrote a series of essays on life in Berrow at the time and who became a keen golfer and long-standing member of the club.

But worst of all was the sand. In those days the dunes had yet to be planted with marram grass and there wasn't a buckthorn bush in sight. With the result that, when a gale blew in from the Bristol Channel, in JH Taylor's words, "the force of the wind cut gorges in the faces of the seaward hills which acted as funnels and the sand poured out like an avalanche … It was heart-breaking to find the greens covered with sand which had to be wheeled away in barrows."

Fate also took a kindly hand in the young professional's career, when Canon Kennard's brother Adam, who was President of the Winchester Golf Club, arranged a challenge match between his professional, the redoubtable Andrew Kirkaldy, three times runner-up in the Open, who was on a six-month secondment to the club, and the young pretender from Burnham, as JH was undoubtedly seen. It was a 36-hole match, 18 on each course. Kirkaldy had the better of things at Winchester, but not by much, finishing 1 up. But amongst the sand, rabbits and worm-casts of Burnham, Taylor was the master, polishing his man off by 4 and 3.

"Well done, laddie, by God you're a guid golfer," said Kirkaldy to his young conqueror as they walked off the final green arm in arm. It was an opinion evidently shared by Adam Kennard. For when Kirkaldy returned to Scotland, Taylor got the call to take his place. Once again, he was in a quandary. "I was sorry to leave Burnham where I had made many friends, but I here make the confession that it was the sand that determined the step. Fighting the sand was a never-ending battle, with it always the winner, and I longed to be somewhere where its ravages were unknown to the same extent."

So JH Taylor left Burnham in October 1892 and would go on to win five Open Championships, as well as doing great work for his fellow golf professionals and becoming one of the best-loved figures the game has ever known. He never lost his affection for Burnham, returning from time to time, as we shall see, to play exhibition matches, and remaining very much a Burnham hero, not least to Ernie Foord.

Taylor's departure left a vacancy as professional which, after a certain H Spinks had come and gone in a week, the Burnham Committee decided to fill by promoting Walter Foord from his job as head green-keeper. Probably Canon Kennard and co felt that with professional challenge matches all the rage and new tournaments springing up almost every summer, they would rather have as a pro someone who would be there all the time, to minister to the members and the course, rather than a celebrity pro who might be away from the club for long periods.

At any event, it was a big step up for a man who, just three years previously, had never touched a golf club in his life, and speaks volumes for his qualities, and indeed for his and his wife Sarah's popularity with the members. Walter Foord was never a 'professional', in the sense of being a champion golfer, as JH Taylor was already, and as his son Ernie would become. He seems to have been more of a head green-keeper, who sold and repaired clubs, while his assistant, a W Johnson who ended up as pro at Clevedon, gave the lessons. Walter Foord is one of the unsung heroes of Burnham and Berrow Golf Club (as it became in 1897). If anyone can be said to have defeated JH Taylor's great adversary, the sand, then it was surely Walter, with all of the planting of the dunes for which he was responsible, not to mention the course extensions in which he was heavily involved, to 18 holes in 1897 and out beyond the church in 1901, and the transformation of the once derided Burnham greens into some of the finest in the land. He must have been quite a character, to cope with all of that blowing sand and the pestilential worms and rabbits, and keep what was no doubt a very demanding membership as happy as it would appear they were.

For the three Foord boys, their father's promotion was a dream come true. Not only could they use the pro shop as a base, but their continued employment, as either caddies or on the course, was as good as guaranteed. They must have loved spending time in the shop, breathing in the intoxicating smells of twine and glue, gutta-percha and leather, hickory and hot iron, and learning all the time: how to judge the whippiness of a shaft, how to match clubheads to shafts, how to produce the perfectly balanced clubs that were needed to get the most out of the capricious gutty balls.

That aptitude, together with his acknowledged skill as a player and an unquenchable enthusiasm for the game, made Ernie one of the most popular of the Burnham tribe of caddies. Like his father, Ernie was not overly deferential to the moustachioed members in their tweed caps, Norfolk jackets and plus twos, but they liked his cheekiness and willingness to offer advice on the line of a putt, or the best way to escape from one of the cavernous bunkers, even if he was only 11 years old.

One member who took a particular shine to the green-keeper's son was a certain Samuel Moses James Woods, probably the most remarkable all-round sportsman ever to have walked the green hills of Somerset. Sammy, as he was always known, was the son of an Irish farmer who had emigrated to Australia during the potato famine, there to make a fortune through his contracting business, building the new roads, railways and docks that a fast-growing country required. Sam had been sent to England to add a bit of old country polish to his Irish-Australian no-nonsense ruggedness and had finished up at Bridgwater, thanks to a business contact of his father's, Gilbert Burrington.

He certainly made his mark. By the time that the new golf course was opened at Burnham, Sam had played cricket as a tearaway fast bowler and hard-hitting middle-order batsman for Australia against England (he would go on to play three tests *for* England), had captained both Somerset and Cambridge University at cricket and earned his first international caps for England at rugby union.

Club members at the autumn meeting, 1898

Sammy Woods is seated, second from the right

He is surely the only man ever to have played rugby for England against Wales in the same year that he played cricket for Australia against England! At school in Brighton, he had represented Sussex at football and would represent Somerset at hockey, football, boxing, billiards and even skittles, as well as being its longest-serving cricket captain (1894-1906).

Sammy Woods

If ever a man could be said to have become a legend, not just in his own lifetime, but in his own playing career, it was Sammy Woods. Six feet tall, broad-shouldered, strong as an ox, with a chin the size of Ayers Rock, Sam was the supreme athlete. He was also a supreme character, as extrovert as you like, as sociable with dustmen as with dukes, never happier than when sharing a bottle of 'pop', as he called it, with team-mates or opponents, whilst singing the night away. Two anecdotes, both related in his autobiography, *My Reminiscences* (an absolute classic), will give you the flavour of the man. The first is from his youth when, every Christmas, the Woods brothers and their father would take a schooner and cruise around the South Sea Islands.

> On one occasion we went to Levuka (Fiji) and were asked to play cricket for the whites against the natives. The natives won the toss, and when I left after the first day's play, the score, as far as I can remember, was 175 for 72. I know I accounted for 25 of them. I think some had come in twice, but they were so alike one couldn't tell t'other from which.

Then there was the time when CI Thornton's England XI came to Cambridge to play the University. As the host captain Sammy decided he ought to offer them some hospitality, so provided hot lobsters, bacon and eggs, cold tongue and beer for breakfast in his rooms. Thornton and his fellow internationals weren't sure that hot lobster was quite the thing on the morning of the second day of a big match, leaving Sammy and his room-mate Gregor MacGregor to tuck in.

> Mac and I didn't have bacon or eggs or cold tongue, as they were lovely birds, those lobsters, washed down with Jesus Audit Ale. The game was continued, and I took all ten wickets against them, and we won by 4 wickets!

Sammy could play any game he cared to turn his hand to and, when the new club opened at Burnham, he decided to have a crack at golf. 1891 was a busy and important cricket season – Somerset's first in the county championship – so he didn't get the chance to visit Burnham until the autumn, where he was straightaway taken under the wing of the young professional, JH Taylor.

Their respective accounts of Sammy's prowess largely concur. At first acquaintance he found the game 'quite easy' (Sammy) to the point where 'he seemed almost to be treating the game with contempt' (JHT). But it didn't last. He developed what Taylor described as 'a vicious slice, whose only alternative was a huge swipe to square leg'. Thereafter, their accounts diverge, with Sammy claiming that advice from his mentor to 'swing at the ball, not hit it as you do in cricket' put him back on the straight and narrow, enabling him to play off a handicap of 2, whereas JHT avers that 'he remained a bad player all his life, a punishment perhaps for his early disdain for a game he never mastered.' I guess the truth is probably somewhere in between.

At any event, the great Sammy Woods became something of a fixture at Burnham and Berrow GC, especially during the winter months when he wasn't cricketing and, later in life, when his cricketing days were over. Word spread quickly among the boy caddies if Sammy was expected. And when the tall, steel-backed figure arrived, stepping out of his cab from the station, a frantic rush would ensue to claim his custom. "Please sir, please sir, can I carry your clubs today?" they would call out, imploringly, as the caddy-master tried to shoo them away from the great man.

"Now just calm down, young 'uns," he would say. "I guess it's Boxer's turn today" – or Eddy's, or Fred's or any one of the dozens of urchin faces looking up adoringly into his smiling blue eyes. But if it was a big game, he would always take Ernie because he knew that, in Ernie, he had a kindred spirit: not just desperately enthusiastic but, for his years, shrewd, calm and assertive enough to insist that he, Sammy, take his iron, even if, to Sammy's ever-optimistic eye, it looked no more than a firmly struck mashie shot.

It was when he was walking down the old third fairway, Ernie at his side, that legend insists Sammy Woods coined the phrase 'tiger country', after one of his right-angled hooks had deposited his ball far out in the wilderness, he declining to look for it on the grounds that "there may be tigers about"! He also had the reputation for what we would now describe as 'gamesmanship' (if not outright cheating!), although it was really more of a form of the Victorian high jinks so beloved by the likes of WG Grace, in which almost anything went as long as there was a good laugh at the end of it.

By way of example, let us take the morning – it was probably a Sunday – when Sammy was playing a foursome, four pints of beer the stake, alongside his great friend Gilbert 'The Croucher' Jessop (who could hit the ball every bit as far as Sammy and a great deal straighter). Ernie Foord was on Woods' bag, while Jackie Johnson, a local ne'er-do-well who came to a sad end, was carrying for Jessop. Sammy had the honour at the short sixth and hit one of his trade-mark slices into what he describes as 'an appalling place'.

"We might have taken ten to get on the green at a one-shot hole!" he would recall. "However, our pals went off to the left, and when we got to our ball, my partner said, 'Lord, look at it.' I said, 'Shut up', picked the ball up, found a nice spot, he laid it dead, I shouted 'Good shot.' We won the hole in 3 to 5."

Sammy had no time for slow play. "I think the present four ball foursome is detrimental to a player's game," he declared. "In fact, I don't think it, I'm sure of it." So when he and Jessop were held up by a slow four in front, and were several times driven into at blind holes by the two ball behind, Sammy got angry. The last straw came at Majuba, when a ball from behind landed on the green just as Sammy was putting out. He determined on revenge. Before leaving the green he placed the intruding ball in the hole and waited for the shouts of triumph from behind. Back at the clubhouse, the happy golfer was informed that the penalty for a hole in one was (as indeed it still is at Burnham) a bottle of whisky, for which JH Taylor charged him 4/6. Only later, as he was going home in the train, was he informed of what had really happened!

Sammy Woods swiped his way happily round Burnham for many years, even serving on the committee from 1912 up to the outbreak of the First World War. He enjoyed the company of the Berrow caddies and admired their remarkable golfing prowess, just as they hero-worshipped the great cricketer.

'From our links,' he would write proudly, 'I suppose we have turned out more young professionals than from any other place in England, what with the Foords, Bradbeers, Days, Whitcombes, Gadds * etc, and a finer set of players one couldn't find. Golf was born in them.'

It was, indeed. The Berrow boys took to golf with a quite remarkable degree of enthusiasm and success. No fewer than 18 of the pre-WW1 Berrow caddies went on to become professionals: Ernie and Fred Foord, at their home club and later in the USA; the three Whitcombe brothers Ernest, Charles and Reg, of whom Reg would win the Open in 1938 at Royal St George's and all three play in the Ryder Cup; the seven Bradbeer brothers – Edwin, James, Charles, Francis, Bob, Ernest and Fred – four of whom qualified for the final two rounds of the 1928 Open Championship; Arthur and Ernie Day; John Pople, who was

The Gadds actually came from Malvern.

head-hunted from Burnham to become pro at Henbury; and Edward and Jack Ham, who became pros at Wells.

There is no single explanation for this phenomenon. Peer rivalry and competitiveness must have played a part. The Whitcombes and Bradbeers lived almost next door to each other, the one family in a cottage (long since demolished) next to the church and the other next to the Wesleyan chapel.

They it was who devised their own caddies' course, with its short holes on the village green and its long holes up on the dunes. It may have been distinctly rough – the greens especially – but it gave them the chance to learn to play, and there was never any shortage of golf-mad youngsters ready to have a game, once they'd finished their caddying for the day. The Foords had the advantage that their father was green-keeper at the club, as indeed did the Whitcombes, once their father Albert had taken over as head green-keeper in the mid 1890s. With the Day brothers, it was the Burnham Ladies Golf Course, constructed by their father Joe on the linksland immediately south of B&B GC in 1901, that provided the opportunity for both work and practice, Arthur eventually going on to serve as pro at Ganton for many happy years.

The boys were fortunate as well in their mentors. As an ex-caddy himself, and not that much older than most of the boys, JH Taylor understood perfectly their hopes, fears and burning ambition. His successor Walter Foord was, of course, a Berrow man made good, thanks to the golf club. And as golf clubs of that era went, Burnham does seem to have been more benevolent than most towards its caddying tribe, thanks to the example set by its President Canon Kennard and members like the visiting golfer, his name sadly lost in the mists of time, who always gave his bag to the unfortunate Jackie Johnson. He was more distressed than anyone when Jackie failed to turn up one day and was eventually found dead from exposure and starvation in the barn near Brean, which was the only home he had.

This isn't to suggest that all was sweetness and light in the relationship between the golf club and the villagers. Just as had been foreseen, on the basis of experience at Westward Ho!, an element among the villagers was deeply hostile to the golf club toffs, encroaching on their grazing and exterminating their rabbits, however many jobs the club might be providing. Right from the start, there was trouble.

'Nightly, villagers damaged greens, befouled holes, uprooted direction posts and did all in their power to ruin the course,' reported Heneage Wheeler. The fact that villagers weren't even allowed to play golf on the course only added to the resentment. Guerrilla warfare went on for years. Matters finally came to a head in early 1908. At the February committee meeting a complaint was received from members of having been 'molested on the course' by Berrow villagers. Worse was to follow in March, when on Sunday 15th the villagers staged a wholesale 'invasion of the links', to the very great inconvenience and annoyance of members and visitors.

The committee's first response was to meet fire with fire. Members were to be asked not to employ as caddies any individuals who were suspected of playing illegally on the links. But by May the tone had changed dramatically. Instead of villagers being barred from the links on pain of loss of livelihood, they were instead to be permitted to play on part of the course (not out beyond the church) on Sundays, provided that their names were given to the club's agent, JH Palmer. Before long, the Berrow Artisans golf club was formed, its members being issued with permits, and a lasting peace established. I wonder if it is not too fanciful to detect the hand of the Foord family in this dramatic change of both policy and outcome. Ernie was by this time club professional, his father Walter was head green-keeper and his mother Sarah looked after the clubhouse. They commanded the respect of both villagers and golf club. If anyone could break what was a deeply damaging deadlock, it was the Foords. And it cannot surely be just coincidence that at the same meeting at which the settlement with the villagers was agreed, the committee also voted to give significant pay increases to both Walter and Sarah Foord. But whoever was responsible, it was a happy outcome. As Heneage Wheeler put it, 'these same misguided miscreants (who had caused all the damage) now became the club's most loyal protectors.'

There was still plenty of work on the course to keep the villagers busy. Despite all the problems with sand, and worms, and rabbits, such was the success of the club that, by the mid-1890s, plans to extend the course to a full 18 holes were being drawn up. Once again, the Westward Ho! professional Charles Gibson was brought in to supervise the work with, once again, Walter Foord as his right-hand man, assisted now by Arthur Whitcombe. The new holes ran from what became the 4th green (the present day 3rd), up the eastern side of the sandhills which separate the present 15th from the 6th on the Channel course. There was then a blind short hole, from the present 5th tee, over high sandhills, to a green in the hollow by the present 14th tee, which was followed by the famous Old Mill hole – sold for housing in the 1970s – over the sandy track with its ancient sea wall, and so back to what had been the 4th green (the present day 15th), along the flat land well to the east of today's 15th fairway.

It was a quirky layout, with plenty of blind shots, daunting carries over towering dunes and punch-bowl greens, but at 4,700 yards it wasn't particularly long, even by the standards of those days, and was regarded – not least by JH Taylor – as being rather too short to challenge the really top players, especially when the rubber-cored Haskell ball appeared on the scene from the early 1900s onwards. So no sooner had the new holes been brought into play than pressure was being applied for a further extension, to take the course out beyond the church, especially now that the early misgivings of the lords of the manor had been dispelled and the club was given the lease of virtually the entire warren.

Walter Foord was the man chosen by the committee to oversee what was a formidable task, and they wanted him to give it his full attention, which meant him giving up his position as professional. To replace him, they decided not to appoint a seasoned professional from, say, Scotland, or even an up-and-coming playing professional, in the mould of JH Taylor, but instead to give the job to Walter's 16-year-old son Ernest. It was an extraordinary vote of confidence in one so young and speaks volumes for Ernie's character, as well as for his undoubted golfing skills. Because, remember, Burnham and Berrow was not just any old provincial golf club. Thanks to the Kennards, and Horace Hutchinson, and JH Taylor, and the challenge matches that he had played there against the likes of James Braid, Burnham now had a national reputation. Ernie Foord, aged 16, with hardly anything in the way of a formal education, was being offered one of the plum jobs in English golf. He must have been a quite remarkable young man, as well as a quite remarkable young golfer.

The extended course
Illustrated Sporting and Dramnatic News, July 1897

2

'A world's record'

Professional golf was still in its infancy when Ernie Foord was appointed as the Burnham professional. There was the Open Championship, of course, in which professionals had been allowed to take part (and had usually won) since it was started in 1860, but it wasn't until the Professional Golfers' Association was formed in 1901 – JH Taylor very much to the fore – that the first professionals-only tournament was established, in the shape of the PGA Championship, better known then and for many years afterwards by the name of its major sponsor, the News of the World. For the rest, professional golf consisted of challenge matches, in which the great golfers of the day pitted themselves either against each other, usually for substantial purses, or sometimes against the leading amateurs, often in the context of the opening of a new course or the extension of an existing one.

In Burnham's case, the opening of the course was marked, as we have seen, by a match between JH Taylor and his old adversary from Royal North Devon, Horace Hutchinson. The club went one better when the course was extended to 18 holes in 1897. This time, it was arranged for the up-and-coming Scottish professional, James Braid, to take on Burnham's favourite professional son, a contest won by Taylor, 2 and 1.

For the 1901 course extension, Burnham decided to aim high. The plan was to stage a Challenge Match between, with all due respect to James Braid, the two greatest golfers of the day, with six Open Championships between them: JH Taylor (1894, 1895 and 1900) and Harry Vardon (1896, 1898 and 1899). However, the commitments of both men meant that this couldn't be played until April 1903, so an alternative had to be found. And what better than to pit Burnham's original Champion golfer against the lad who many of the members were convinced would eventually follow in his footsteps? The ever-obliging JH said yes to the idea, and Ernie Foord, one year into his professional career and just 17 years old, could scarcely believe his luck.

The match was played on the day that the course extension was opened, 27 April 1901, and a reporter (probably the editor) from *Golf Illustrated* was there to watch it. This is his account:

> A very large number of spectators assembled to witness this match on April 27 to inaugurate the opening of the 18-hole course and were rewarded by a brilliant all-round display by the Champion, who played with his accustomed deadly accuracy.
>
> His opponent, the club professional, a lad of only 17, suffered greatly from nervousness, especially at the start, and consequently did not bring out his usual strong game in approaching and putting. He, however, drove a low ball throughout from the tee and on two or three occasions out-drove the champion. The mashie play of the latter was enough to demoralise the strongest of players, especially during the latter part of each round, as will be seen from the scores below. The weather was cold, with a fairly strong wind going out, which accounted for the somewhat high scoring at some of the long holes. The champion gained an advantage of 7 up on the first round, and eventually won the match by 8 up and 6 to play.
>
> Taylor won the first hole in 3 to 4 after a very fine straight drive, Foord's approach being short. The second and third holes were halved. The fourth was won by the Champion, who laid his ball dead with a (fine) mashie shot out of the bunker short of the green. The 5th and 6th were both halved. The seventh was won by Taylor in 2, with a long putt, his drive being on the green. Foord's drive at the 8th was slightly pulled, which put him in the background; he, however, recovered himself grandly with a fine long 4th which laid his ball practically dead; he, however, missed the

putt, losing the hole in 6 to 5. The 9th (a full drive over a large high sandhill) was halved in 3 after two long tee shots and approaches. The 10th and 11th were both halved in 5 each. Foord won the 12th and 13th by good putting, thereby reducing Taylor's lead to 2 up. After this, however, the champion's play was simply irresistible, he taking the last five holes in succession with scores of 3, 3, 4, 2, 4, which left him 7 up on the round.

After lunch, Foord played with much greater confidence at the first 8 holes, his score out being level with the champion's, and he won the first, third, fifth and sixth, the latter taking the second and fourth. The 7th and 8th were both halved in 3 and 5 respectively, Foord playing an exceptionally fine second at the latter. Taylor won the 9th in 2 after a full mashie shot off his drive which laid his ball dead, Foord being bunkered to the left of the green off a pulled drive. The Champion made a magnificent drive and second shot at the tenth (a hole 476 yards long), the latter being only about 30 yards short of the green, and took the hole in 5 to 7, Foord playing out of bounds with his third. The 11th was halved in 3. Taylor, however, won the 12th in 5 to Foord's 6 thereby winning the match by 8 up with 6 to play. He was also 4 up on the bye, holing the last 6 holes in 20, the deadly accuracy of his approaches being simply marvellous. Par of green 82.

Ernie had been beaten but had certainly not been humiliated, by his hero. To have come out so strongly in the afternoon after the battering he had taken from the remorseless accuracy of Taylor's mashie play over the closing holes of the morning round showed great spirit, as well as great skill. His scores of 79 and 74 were disappointing, especially when set against Taylor's 71 and 67, but bear in mind that last sentence in the Golf Illustrated report: **'Par of green 82.'** The story of the round was not 'Nervous Ernie crushed' so much as 'Taylor's brilliance too much for gallant young Burnham pro'.

JH Taylor v Ernie Foord

Burnham & Berrow Golf Club

27 April 1901

Morning		Afternoon	
Taylor	Foord	Taylor	Foord
3	4	4	3
4	4	3	4
6	6	5	4
6	7	5	6
4	4	4	3
3	3	3	2
2	3	3	3
5	6	5	5
3	3	2	4
36	*40*	*34*	*34*
5	5	5	7
5	5	3	3
5	4	5	6
4	3	4	5
3	4	2	3
3	4	4	4
4	5	4	4
2	4	2	3
4	5	4	5
35	*39*	*33*	*40*
71	**79**	**67**	**74**

JH Taylor v Ernie Foord, 27 April 1901

(top) Taylor driving from the 1st tee
(bottom) Taylor driving from the 4th tee

(top) Foord driving from the 5th tee
(bottom) Foord driving from the 6th tee

JH Taylor v Ernie Foord, 27 April 1901

(top) Taylor playing brassie to 8th hole
(bottom) Some of the spectators, with the 11th tee in the background

(top) The 14th green
(bottom) Foord putting on the 16th green

JH Taylor v Harry Vardon, 25 April 1903

This was the match originally arranged to celebrate the extension of the course in April 1901. Golf Illustrated reported: 'Enthusiasts from all parts of the West of England assembled in large numbers to witness what proved to be a ding-dong tussle from start to finish.'

Taylor's defeat by 3 & 2 was his first on the Burnham links.

(above) Match referee Herbert Fowler (left), Harry Vardon (centre) and JH Taylor (right of centre)
(opposite, top) Vardon putting on the 14th green
(opposite, bottom) Taylor playing out of a bunker at the 18th

The first decade of the twentieth century – the Edwardian 'golden age' – was a particularly happy period in the history of Burnham and Berrow GC. The course was improving all the time, as the tough grasses planted so painstakingly on the dunes by Walter Foord and his team of green-keepers began to bring the sand under control. The editor of *Golf Illustrated* thoroughly approved of the 1901 extension:

> The new holes will bring the course up to the standard of a first-class course, and it will be of a general excellence attained only by the very best seaside courses. The course as now arranged will provide a splendid test of the game in all its departments and will probably have the finest 18th hole on any course. The putting-greens are lovely and the air is celebrated for its health-giving qualities.

None of this happened by accident. The club was blessed with a benevolent President in Canon Kennard, an efficient secretary in Thomas Holt and a sensible committee, and the quality of the golfing experience was already such as to attract any number of top-class players as members or visitors. They included men such as Herbert Fowler, once a Somerset cricketer, now a budding golf architect, Captain Prideaux-Brune, Captain JS Armstrong and GD Barne, scratch players all, and perhaps the best golfer of the lot of them, Hugh Alison, who would go on to become Burnham's resident golf architect and, as such, with Harry Colt, would give us the great golf course that Burnham became.

National recognition was not long in coming. In 1906 Burnham was chosen to host the Ladies Amateur Championship and the Ladies' Home Internationals, which preceded it. The event was pronounced a great success, with around 3,000 spectators turning up to watch Alice Kennion from Brighton defeat the reigning champion Bertha Thompson 4/3 in the final. Burnham did not, of course, allow lady members at that stage in its history (the first 'lady associate members' were elected in 1931, and ladies were not permitted in the lounge bar until 1949!), although there was a reciprocal arrangement with the

Burnham Ladies Golf Club next door, for ladies to play the men's course with a member and vice versa.

Even as a teenager, Ernie was an outstanding teacher of the game, as well as being a quite brilliant player, and the keener members liked nothing better than to go out for a full round to watch, listen and learn from their precocious professional. On 23 June 1903 the privilege of playing with him fell to a Mr GH Hunt. And privilege it was, for Ernie proceeded to break his own course record (of 68) by going round in 65. But even better was to follow a few days later on 1 July, when Mr JM Warren was Ernie's playing partner.

Ernie made just about the best possible start, with three 3s. In those days the first hole measured 224 yards, played over the sandhills to the left of the present-day first fairway, to a green close to the track which runs along the northern edge of the practice ground. It was a fine, calm, sunny day, and Ernie could reach the green comfortably with his driver. The second was another short bogey 4, of 247 yards, played from a sandy mound beyond and some distance back from the first green, to a fairway some 50 yards short of what is now the first green, and so over another ridge of dunes to a green in hollow beyond and to the right of the present second tee. The very longest hitters could reach the green in one, but the guardian sandpits and dunes made going for it a risky endeavour. Ernie, as confident in his chipping and putting as he must have been, probably laid up short of the hazards and then lobbed the ball close with his niblick. The third hole was rather longer, at 350 yards, and was essentially a slightly shorter version of the present 2nd, to a green in the hollow to the right of the present green. Again, for a golfer as accomplished as Ernie Foord, it was no more than a good drive, a pitch and a single putt.

So far, so straightforward, but now the holes got tougher. The 4th in 1903 was essentially today's third, albeit played from the lower tee (which is now used in the winter for the 17th), and at 366 yards, required two good blows. Ernie played it conventionally in bogey 4. The 5th hole was even more of a challenge. At 456 yards it was the second longest on the course, played from a tee to the right of the present 3rd green, to a fairway of humps and hollows, along the eastern side of the line of sandhills, over the sandy crevasse known as 'the kitchen' (which was a lot more fearsome then than now), with a blind third shot to a green in the deep natural hollow between the present day 4th and 14th greens. This was actually one of early Burnham's more forgiving greens. On one occasion, in the 36-hole medal Tradesmen's Cup, Heneage Wheeler, by his own account, played the hole twice in one day without having to putt. On both occasions, his purposely overhit approach ran back down the slope behind the pin and so into the hole! Ernie Foord had no such luck and had to settle for a 5.

Then came two short holes: the 6th was played from the existing 5th tee, over the high sandhills to the right, to a green in another deep hollow by what is now the 14th tee. It was completely blind and, at 172 yards, required a good hit with a cleek (3 iron) or even a spoon (3 wood). But, as with the previous hole, a ball which reached the green would tend to gather towards the hole. Ernie made his 3. The tee for the 7th was roughly where the 13th green is now, diagonally across a line of sandhills to another deep hollow, only recently filled in the re-modelling of the present 6th; hence its name of 'Crater'. Ernie hit his mid-iron to 20 feet and holed the putt for a 2.

The 8th was a tough bogey 4 of 410 yards, played from a tee close to the bridle path to a hog's back of a fairway well to the right of the present day 7th, and so to a green level with the fairway bunker on today's 7th. Ernie was happy enough to settle for a par 4. The first nine concluded with another blind short hole, Spion Kop as it was known (betraying, as with Majuba, the Boer War experiences of many of Burnham's early members). It was played from west to east over the sandhills which separate today's 7th fairway from 11th green, and represented a good chance of gaining a shot on its bogey 4 if the wind was off the sea. Ernie put what was probably a brassie shot on the green and two-putted for his 3, to be out in 30, 5 better than bogey.

Mr JM Warren, who had been playing steadily enough off his handicap of 5, found himself five down and could barely control his excitement at the golf he had witnessed from his playing partner. "I might," he thought to himself, "be part of history!"

But now for the real test. If several of the holes on Burnham's outward nine could be described as quirky, the run of holes from the 10th to the 13th represented nothing more or less than flat-out good golf. At 476 yards, the 10th, the Church hole as it came to be known, was the longest on the course. Three long straight blows were required to reach the green, protected as it was by out of bounds on either hand, reinforced by elm trees up by the green. Ernie was happy with his 5. The 11th, the Old Mill hole, was what we would nowadays call Burnham's 'signature hole'. There is a splendid photograph of JH Taylor driving here in his match against Braid in 1898, the tee set just in front of the remains of the mill. Later, the tee was moved slightly higher up into the dunes, but from either location the key to the hole was the drive, and how much of the sandy track – known, with a certain lack of originality as 'the Old Kent Road' – to cut off so as to shorten the route to the green. This was the hole sold off by the club to clear its overdraft back in the 1970s, of which the less said the better!

To put one's ball on the track, with its deep ruts and steep bank, was to court disaster. Ernie cleared it comfortably and made his 4. So to the 12th, which was essentially a shorter version of today's 15th as played from the championship tee. At 410 yards it was long and challenging, played over broken ground to a green which, then as now, was protected by a tall sand-hill. Ernie judged his second shot perfectly and was able to watch it kick left down the slope in front of the green, to finish close. His approach putt shaved the hole, but that was another 4 in the bag. Better still was to come at the next, his 13th, today's 16th, albeit with a sandy waste all up the right hand side, running down to what was then a cavernous bunker, made famous as 'Hutchinson's bunker' for the travails that the great amateur had once endured therein. But, at just over 300 yards, all it really needed was a straight drive and a firm pitch. Ernie made no mistake and this time holed his putt for a three.

So four holes, three of them over 400 yards, had been played by Ernie Foord in 5, 4, 4, 3, against a bogey score of 6, 5, 5, 5. He had picked up 5 shots against the card, and this on Burnham's toughest stretch. But this was no time for resting on laurels. Majuba – unquestionably

Burnham's most famous short hole – loomed ahead. Named, with entirely conscious irony, after the hill on which the British army had suffered a shattering defeat against the Boers in 1881, the hole had recently been re-modelled and was now played from a tee to the right of the 13th green (today's blue tee at the third) over the top of the giant sand-hill on which the 3rd and 17th tees now stand – which was a good 20 feet taller in those days – to a green just beyond and to the left of today's 17th forward tee. It was a daunting hole, for sure, but not a particularly good one, even by the standards of nineteenth century golf architecture. You picked the line, hit and hoped for the best. At 190 yards in its revised format, only the longest hitters could hope to put their tee shot on the green. Here Ernie made his only real mistake, pulling his tee shot into the dunes to the left of the green and just failing with his putt for a 3.

Tom Holt driving at the Majuba hole

Burnham's last four holes were very different in 1903 to the ones we know today. The 15th was a dog-leg left bogey 4 of 280 yards, out into the sand-hills beyond today's 17th green, almost to the eastern boundary of the warren. The 16th, a short bogey 4 of 205 yards, came back at an angle of 90 degrees, to a green which must have been just short of the last and deepest of the hollows to the left of today's 18th fairway. At 122 yards, the 17th was the shortest hole on the course and one of the easiest, played south to north from a tee on the sandhill to the left of the present 18th fairway to a green tucked in under the big dunes, more or less where a drive hit long and left off today's 18th tee would finish. The finishing hole was essentially a shorter version of our present 18th, albeit with a big sand ridge running across it some 90 yards from the green – removed by Harry Colt in his remodelling of the course after the First World War – which made the second shot yet another blind one, on what was, at 345 yards, a suitably challenging final hole.

Ernie Foord played those last four holes in 4, 4, 2, 3. He might have hoped to shave off a stroke or two more from bogey, but he had avoided a card-wrecking disaster, and 33 on the homeward stretch had left him with a well-nigh unbelievable 63 – a little matter of 15 strokes better than bogey. He was a happy man as he walked off the 18th green, comfortable in his own mind that there was only one man (apart from himself, of course) who was likely ever to be able to beat such a score around Burnham's sandy wastes, and that was the great JH Taylor. As for Mr Warren, well he went rushing into the clubhouse to tell anyone he could find about the quite remarkable round of golf he had just witnessed. "I doubt we'll ever see the like of it again," he crowed. "The boy's a golfing genius!"

The editor of *Golf Illustrated* evidently agreed. Describing Ernie as Burnham and Berrow's 'brilliant young professional' and at pains to emphasise that the course had been played at its full length, from the medal tees, he called the round 'extraordinary' and suggested it might 'possibly be a world's record'. Whether it was or not, we will never know. It is perfectly possible that lower scores had been recorded on shorter, easier courses. Par today for the course that Ernie played would be 66, including 3 par threes of over 200 yards. Bogey, which was a generous version of par which each club set for itself, was 78, although in 1908, the Burnham Committee decided that a 'scratch return' – the sort of score that a golfer of Ernie Foord's quality might expect to take, day in, day out, given reasonable weather – was 75. But, taking everything into account – the equipment (most notably the gutty balls, which were so much more difficult than their rubber-cored successors), the cavernous bunkers, the blind holes, the sandy wastes which awaited any shot seriously off-line, the (by today's standards) less than perfect greens and the fact that Ernie probably played in a tie and Norfolk jacket – a strong case can be made that 63 over the course as it was in 1903 is the equivalent of maybe 58 or 59 over Burnham as it is today.

Outside the pro shop, Ernie, pint of beer in hand, a big smile on his broad face, was surrounded by the boy caddies. "Cor, Ern," one of them piped up, "you'll be beating old JH in the championship next up. I reckon you'm the greatest golfer Somerset ev ever 'ad." And to that point, he certainly was.

The only sad thing about Ernie Foord's course record 63 was that it would stand for only seven years, before the course was once again re-modelled and extended. What a shame that his card seems to have disappeared. Framed, signed and with a photograph of Burnham's triumphant young professional, it would make a handsome addition to the memorabilia on display in the clubhouse.

3

Ernie in The Open

Ernie Foord played in eleven Open Championships without, it must be said, making the impact that his talents deserved. His first attempt was at Muirfield in 1901. He was only 17 and had never travelled beyond the boundaries of Somerset, let alone the 430 miles that separates Burnham from Muirfield. But the club was keen that their outstanding young prospect should try his skill against the very best, to the extent of not only allowing him a week off from his duties but donating £10 towards his travelling expenses. The other factor in the equation was his old friend JH Taylor, the defending champion, no less, after his third Open victory at St. Andrews the previous June. He had written to Walter during the winter, not only encouraging him to allow Ernie to make the trip but promising, as the worldly-wise golfer he had now become, to keep a watchful eye on the youngster.

Confident lad though he undoubtedly was, it was still a very nervous Ernie who climbed aboard the 7.51 from Highbridge, his bag of clubs slung over his shoulder, for the long journey, first via Bristol to Birmingham and then on a through carriage to Edinburgh, for the final change to Longniddry and Muirfield. By the time he reached his bed and breakfast in Gullane that evening, he was dog-tired, not just from the journey but from all the conversations he'd had with fellow travellers who, once they'd spotted his clubs in the rack, could not resist either relating their own golfing experiences or asking Ernie about his.

The next morning dawned sunny and as breezy as you would expect on the East coast of Scotland, and Ernie's spirits began to lift as he walked to the course, apprehension giving way to excitement at the prospect of mixing with all of the great men of golf. In those days, the Open was not just golf's pre-eminent championship, it was a great gathering of the professional golfing clan – a 'carnival, where they (the pros) may fraternize with each other and perhaps in so doing advance their material interests', as the *Glasgow Herald*'s golf correspondent rather snootily put it.

As promised, the familiar, four-square figure of JH was there to greet him with a broad smile and outstretched hand. Alongside stood the other great champion, Harry Vardon, whom Ernie had met when he'd played an exhibition match at Burnham four years previously. "You'll recall this young fellow, Harry," said JH. "He's become quite a player, by all accounts. In fact, if I could putt like him, I reckon I might be almost as good a golfer as you!"

It was a great moment in the young man's life: to be treated as an equal by the two greatest golfers ever to have played the game. Life must suddenly have seemed very sweet. There was only one thing bothering him, and that was his game. He could still hole the putts, but his long game was ragged, and he knew all about Muirfield's fearsome reputation and the greens that year were frighteningly fast.

There was no qualifying in those days. Opens were played over 72 holes on the Wednesday and Thursday of Open week, with the preceding days given over to practice. Out of a total entry of, in this case, 101, the top 60 and ties after the first two rounds would go on to battle it out over the final two rounds. Ernie thoroughly enjoyed his practice rounds and made many new friends over the first couple of days, but when it came to the real thing he was overcome with nerves and failed to do himself any sort of justice. Two rounds of 89 meant that he missed the cut for the final 36 holes by some margin. He stayed to watch the final day, and his disappointment was complete when his hero, JH, could only manage third behind Vardon and the home favourite, a certain James Braid, who won the first of his five Opens by three shots with a total of 309, to the unmitigated delight of a huge, and hugely partisan, Scottish crowd.

"When a Scottish success is registered even in a minor competition the amount of enthusiasm that is engendered is something to be seen and remembered," JH Taylor remarked. "Compared with the tepid demonstration of an English crowd, it gives one the impression that Bannockburn is being fought once again."

Ernie missed the 1902 Open, at Hoylake, won famously by Sandy Herd using the revolutionary, as it soon became, Haskell ball. The club had already given him a week off, to learn club-making and repairing at St Andrews and that, they decided, was quite enough generosity for one year. But he was back for Prestwick in 1903, with its out of bounds all the way down the left of the first fairway and those famous stone walls, and he did pretty well. Opening rounds of 80 and 84 meant that he qualified comfortably for the final day. The early summer had been hot in the West of Scotland, leaving the course parched and the greens fast and bumpy. But that, of course, played to Ernie's greatest strengths, on and around the greens, and 81, 82 on the final day lifted him to 33rd with a total of 327. That was the small matter of 27 shots behind Harry Vardon's winning 300, but then, as even JH Taylor was prepared to acknowledge, Vardon at his best was in a different class. What made his win even more remarkable was that he was already showing the first symptoms of the tuberculosis which would plague him for the remainder of his career. Shortly after the championship had finished, he was carted off to hospital and it would be another eight years before he won another Open.

There was another Burnham golfer at that 1903 Open, the amateur and former Somerset cricketer Herbert Fowler. He was in his late 40s by now, but had finished a highly creditable 26th in the 1900 Open at St Andrews and, tall and strong as he was, could still drive the ball almost as far as James Braid. He didn't have such a good championship at Prestwick, failing by some margin to qualify, but then his mind was probably elsewhere – at Walton Heath in Surrey, where he was hard at work turning an unpromising stretch of heathland into one of the most famous courses in England. His triumph there brought many other commissions, including the two Berkshire courses, Southerndown, Royal Lytham and St Anne's, Aberdovey and Saunton East, where his 17th hole (16th as it is now) was adjudged by Bernard Darwin to be the finest 17th hole in England.

When Burnham decided, a few years later, that it was time for their course to be extended and re-modelled, Fowler was the obvious man for the job. He it was who gave us the old 6th, as well as the 11th and the 18th (very much as they are today) and who swept away the criss-cross of shortish holes beyond today's 17th green. Harry Colt would, of course, go on to complete the transformation after the war, but Fowler has left a lasting imprint.

But we digress. I daresay Herbert Fowler had a kindly word for young Ernie when their paths crossed on the practice ground or the course (not in the clubhouse, of course – that was for amateurs only), and I daresay it gave Ernie an extra glow of pleasure to have shown one of Burnham's most illustrious members a clean pair of heels. The following year, at Sandwich, he had more congenial Burnham company, in the shape of his near contemporary James Bradbeer, the second oldest of the seven Bradbeer brothers, by now the professional at Finchley in North London. From then until the war, he and Ernie played together in five Opens, James eventually having marginally the better record, his best performance being tied 7th at Hoylake in 1913, when JH Taylor won a famous victory in a storm of wind and rain.

Neither of them enjoyed their first visits to Sandwich very much. The weather was cold and windy, the rough was knee-high and had been grown in almost to the edge of the narrow fairways, and neither survived beyond qualifying. Both of them stayed on to watch the final two rounds, Braid setting the early pace with a record 69 – the first time that 70 had been beaten in the Open. But in the final round, it was Jack White who led the way, matching Braid's score to finish on 296. Mistakenly thinking that he needed a four at the last to tie, Braid played safe and duly got it, only to discover that he had been misinformed. Both were among the early starters, and that seemed to be that. Out on the course JH Taylor had other ideas. He needed a 67 to tie and, in a round which he recalls vividly in his autobiography, he failed by a whisker. At the 16th and 17th, putts for birdies shaved the hole but stayed out, leaving him needing a three at the par four 18th – a hole which, minus the bunkers down the left, is very much now as it was then – to force a play-off.

'My mashie shot to the green I tried to work against the slope, but pushed it over-much up the hill, ten yards away from the hole. I can see that last putt as I write. It was a dusty, dry, dropper with a yard borrow from the right. I gave it a firm chance and a few feet from the hole it looked to be in, but again touching the rim on the borrowed side it slipped a foot past, finishing on the left side. I had failed by the narrowest possible margin.'

His score of 68 was a new Open record, but that was little consolation, either for JH or for his two proteges, watching, agonised, by the final green as their hero was so cruelly denied. It must have been a very long journey home for all of them.

Ernie found himself back on familiar territory for the 1905 Open at St Andrews, where he had spent a week learning club-making in Forgan's Shop in 1902. He played well, under tough conditions, with half a gale blowing on the first day and lightning fast greens. Scores of 85, 86 on that first day may not sound particularly impressive, but not a single player beat 80 in the first round, and the qualifying cut fell at 172, leaving 95 competitors to battle it out over the final two rounds. Ernie's 84 and 83 were good enough to lift him to joint 24th on 338, a distant 20 shots more than Braid's winning total of 318, and even that was 22 shots more than Jack White had taken at Sandwich. JH Taylor finished strongly, with 78 and 80, but again had to be content with a share of second place, as a huge crowd carried their local hero shoulder-high from the final green.

For company at St Andrews, Ernie had Charles Gibson, the Westward Ho! professional who had not only laid out Burnham's original nine holes and advised on its subsequent extension but had also recommended JH Taylor as the club's first professional. Although most famous as a club-maker, Gibson was a fine golfer who served as Royal North Devon's professional for a remarkable 44 years, from 1888 to 1932. He entered the Open only sporadically, and this was the last time he qualified for the final two rounds, finishing 10 shots adrift of Ernie on 348. The pair of them, and JH Taylor, of course, no doubt talked much of their early days at Burnham over a dram or two when the Championship was over – JH probably in need of some liquid consolation, having yet again come second!

For 1906 the Open returned to Muirfield, and so did Ernie Foord. This was another Braid year, and no prizes for guessing who came second! Ernie started brightly, his 78 leaving him just five shots off the first round lead, but he slipped to 84 in the afternoon, which was still comfortably good enough to qualify, eventually finishing tied 30th in another Open of high winds and fast greens. Braid finished, according to Andrew Kirkaldy, 'like a roarin' lion' with a 73 to claim his third Open, evidently not in the least bit hampered by the thick tweed suit in which he is pictured driving from Muirfield's first tee.

Over the Opens of 1907 and 1908, played respectively at Hoylake and Prestwick, it is as well to draw a veil. Ernie played in both but failed to qualify in either. It was a much happier story in 1909, when the Open visited, for the first and so far only time, the links of the Royal Cinque Ports GC at Deal. Not only did Ernie achieve his best finish yet in the Championship, rounds of 77, 80, 81 and 76 leaving him tied 21st, but his hero JH Taylor produced some blistering golf to triumph by six clear shots over Braid and Tom Ball. After the sketchiest of starts – 41 for his opening nine holes – he just got better and better. 'For the next three rounds he played with his most unvarying and brilliant accuracy,' wrote Bernard Darwin. 'Taylor, when he wins nearly always wins easily. He takes on one of his most irresistible moods and leaves his field like a streak of lightning.' Ernie wasn't there to cheer JH as he holed a three-yard putt on the 18th for the win, as he was still out on the course, but he knew full well what the roar that went up must signify, and it inspired him to that closing 76.

The weather for the 1910 Open at St Andrews was atrocious – as filthy as anything that the Bristol Channel can throw at Burnham and Berrow. In fact, the weather was so bad that no play was possible on the first day and the Championship extended by a day in consequence. The wind was so strong that the eventual winner, James Braid, took to using heavier than normal golf balls in the hope of preventing them being blown around on the greens! Under the circumstances Ernie's score of 317, for a share of 28th place, was a more than respectable return, as he finished alongside the familiar figure of John Sherlock against whom he had played an exhibition match to mark the extension of the North Wilts club near Devizes a couple of years previously. Sherlock was the Oxford University professional, a tough and experienced international

Harry Vardon (left) and James Braid, winners of 11 Open Championships between 1896 and 1914

golfer, and he had comfortably prevailed 5/4. For Ernie there was the consolation that he and his father had the better of a fourball match against Sherlock and the club captain, a Mr Morrison, in the afternoon.

For 1911 the Championship was back in the far south-east of England at Royal St George's. It was not a particularly popular choice with the professionals, given that most of the limited accommodation in Sandwich itself had been taken by the tradesmen setting up their stalls at the course, which meant that many of the pros had to find rooms in Deal and travel to the course by train. The situation was not helped by the fact of a record entry of 226, meaning that the first two rounds were spread over two days, with the top 60 going on to play the usual two rounds on the final day. Nor was it a successful expedition for Ernie Foord, opening rounds of 80 and 81 leaving him three shots outside the qualifying mark of 158. But at least he had the consolation of being able to support his friend, fellow Berrow caddie and former assistant pro Ernest Whitcombe, who had got the job of professional at Came Down in Dorset the previous year and was playing in his first Open at the age of just 20.

The pair had known each other all their lives. Ernest's mother Bessie had succeeded Ernie's mother Sarah as stewardess at Burnham in 1902, while Ernest himself had been so respected by Ernie and the Burnham Committee as to have been appointed acting caddy master in 1908, at the age of 17. With all due respect to Charles Gibson at Westward Ho! they were generally regarded as the two best players among the West of England pros and the previous summer had led the field in the regional qualifying competition for the *News of the World* matchplay championship, now in its eighth year and second only to the Open in prestige. In the qualifier at Parkstone, it was Ernest who had the better of things, seeing off his rival by four shots. But in the main event at Sunningdale it was Ernie who had the longer run, surviving into the third round after Ernest had been knocked out in the first. But it was emphatically Ernest who came out on top in that Sandwich Open, opening with a 77 and finishing with a 76, for a total of 318 and a share of 33rd place. Not bad for a 20-year-old in only his second big tournament.

And so to Ernie Foord's final appearance at an Open Championship, at Prestwick in 1914. His family commitments and the ever-increasing demands of an expanding pro shop at Burnham meant that he missed Ted Ray's win at Muirfield in 1912 and JH's final Open victory at Hoylake in 1913, which was a shame given that Ernie was probably at the peak of his golfing powers at around this time. The weather was fine and sunny on the Ayrshire coast, the greens keen and the crowd, especially in the afternoons, enormous and, according to an aggrieved JH Taylor, 'insatiable in its desire to push forward and see everything that was going on.' Bernard Darwin, reporting the Championship for *The Times*, wrote that 'the links now presented the appearance of Derby Day.'

But Ernie Foord, with his extrovert streak, rather enjoyed all the noise, bustle and, above all, attention. He opened with two steady rounds of 82, 81 to qualify comfortably and finished with something of a blaze of glory with a 76, for a share of 19th place, his best Open finish. But he wasn't the only one-time Berrow caddy to feature prominently on Prestwick's crowded links. James Bradbeer also had his best Open so far, to finish joint 14th, although it was Ernest Whitcombe, with an opening 74, who caught Bernard Darwin's eye:

> Among the minor lights there was, as may be seen, a number of thoroughly sound, good scores, but nothing to suggest an upheaval of form at the end of three more rounds. The best of them was a 74 by young Whitcombe, who played so well in the *News of the World* tournament. He is a natural, easy player with plenty of power and dash, who wastes no time over the game.

Praise indeed.

However, the story of that Open was the duel fought out between the defending champion JH Taylor and his old friend and rival Harry Vardon, by now recovered from his TB but suffering all sorts of agonies on the greens. Vardon set the early pace and was two shots ahead after the first day. As luck would have it, the two were drawn together for the final two rounds, something which, according to Taylor, neither of them relished. Even so, Taylor came charging back with a 74 of grim determination, earning himself a two-shot lead at the start of the final round. But a rushed lunch left him flustered for the start of the final round, a short putt which would have extended his lead to four was missed on the very first green, and at the third, the Cardinal, in a portent of things to come, 'a lunatic-looking youth clicked an infernal camera only a few yards away', with Taylor at the top of his backswing. Thoroughly disconcerted, he took a five there to Vardon's four, drove into a bunker at the next, then fluffed his recovery into the Pow Burn, the eventual seven effectively ending his hopes of a 6th Open. His bitterness at the behaviour of the crowd was still raw nearly thirty years later, when he came to write his autobiography, and it was a bitterness undoubtedly shared, on his friend and mentor's behalf, by Ernie Foord.

As Open Championship records go, Ernie Foord's is by no means the most impressive: 11 appearances, six times qualifying for the final two rounds, best finish tied 19th, lowest 18-hole score 76 (at Deal in 1909 and Prestwick in 1914), lowest total 314 at Deal. Quite why he only produced his best form so rarely on the biggest stage, we will never know. But it would not be unfair to conclude that he was probably twice the golfer on his home links at Burnham as he was anywhere else.

4

A professional's life

'The Golden Age' is how we like to think of Edwardian England, and it was certainly that for Burnham and Berrow Golf Club and its young professional. The golf boom of the 1890s continued into the new decade. The exhibition match between Taylor and Vardon in 1903, followed by the hosting of the Ladies Championship in 1906, had put the club very firmly on the golfing map and numbers both of members and visitors increased steadily. The 1901 changes to the course had been well-received, but almost no sooner had they been completed than talk began of further improvements. Initially, attention was focused on the new 8th hole, and the marshy ground all up its left-hand side (roughly where the rhyne is today). Under the leadership of the formidable Major Archdale, Walter Foord and his green-staff were charged with raising the level of the fairway to improve the drainage. That evidently didn't solve the problem, for by June 1908 we find the committee approving a plan, drawn up by Archdale and his surveyor, JH Palmer, to dig a 15-foot-wide ditch, three feet deep, to take surplus water at high tide and so into a pond to the right of what is now the 7th tee.

But it wasn't only Archdale who was determined to take the course to a new level. Captain in 1907 and 1908 (by virtue of golfing prowess, as was the custom in those early days) was Hugh Alison, who had already developed the enthusiasm for golf course architecture which would reach its full flowering in his eventual partnership with Harry Colt. And in Herbert Fowler he and Archdale had the perfect man to turn their dreams for Burnham into reality, long-time club member that he was, and renowned course architect that he had become.

The opportunity that they had been waiting for came in 1909 when, after protracted negotiations, the Lords of the Manor agreed to offer the club a 99-year lease covering the entire 210 acres of the Warren.

The way was now open to extend the course northwards, so paving the way to scrapping the unsatisfactory criss-cross of shortish holes between Majuba and the 18th. Fowler had already been working on plans to do precisely that and, within a month of the Committee taking up the offer of the lease, his report was accepted.

Surprisingly perhaps, he recommended no changes to the first three holes, all of them shortish par 4s (although a new green had been created at the second). It was from the 7th onwards that he made his mark. The green for that hole was moved 100 yards or so northwards, from the line of the bridle path to the right of what is now the 7th tee, so creating the hole that older Burnham members remember as the 6th, which disappeared in the changes of the late 1970s, when its fairway was needed for the new 13th. That was followed by an extended 8th hole, along much the same line as today's 7th and a new 400-yard 9th hole, much closer to the dunes on the right than today's 8th, so as to steer clear of the marshiest ground.

Fowler's 10th took both its name – Spion Kop – and its nature – a long par 3/bogey 4 over the ridge of sandhills, with the prevailing wind off the sea behind – from its immediate predecessor, the green being pretty much today's 10th. The new 11th was essentially today's hole and that was followed by Fowler's only fall from grace, a short hole, from a tee to the right of the 11th green (still visible) to a green to the left of the present 12th fairway. The golfer then had to trek back the best part of 200 yards to the tee for the long Church hole. The next four holes were largely unchanged, barring their numbering, (11, 12, 13 and 14 becoming 14, 15, 16 and 17), the round finishing with the splendid 440-yard par four that we play today. No time was wasted in making the changes, for the new course was in play by the spring of 1910, with a bogey of 81: 42 out, 39 back, although what was known in those days as a 'scratch return' would probably have been a couple of shots lower. It was certainly now a fine test of golf.

Changes were afoot in the clubhouse and the pro shop as well. To coincide with the 1901 course extension, the committee stumped up £100 for a new pro shop for their new young pro, as well as an office for the caddy-master and a cottage for the green-keeper. One of the

The course in 1901

The course in 1910

most important elements of a pro's job in those days was club making and repairing, something which Ernie had picked up the basics of from watching his father at work during the 1890s. But he was very far from being the expert club-maker that the membership would have expected in their pro, and it was very much to the club's credit that they paid for Ernie to spend a week learning club-making in the renowned Forgan's Shop at St Andrews in 1902. Ernie was evidently a fast learner, for he soon acquired a reputation as one of the finest club-makers in England. The surviving examples of his work are precisely crafted, finely balanced and beautifully proportioned: the sort of clubs that would make even the most average golfer feel that he could play a few shots on picking them up.

Besides what might be called 'standard' clubs, a professional was also expected to make clubs to order: a copy of a member's favourite club which had been broken beyond repair, perhaps, or a club to a member's own design, or maybe a club 'guaranteed' to be socket-proof. Down at Royal North Devon, Charles Gibson had helped make a name for himself by creating what he called 'fishing rod drivers', with extra long shafts, whilst niblicks could come in almost every conceivable shape or size. Two of the Ernie Foord clubs on display in the cabinet in the club dining room are 'bulgers' – a driver and a brassie – so called because each has a slightly convex face, intended to reduce backspin and so provide more run, but which must have been fiendishly difficult for the average player to middle.

A socket head bulger driver created by Ernie Foord

65

*An Ernie Foord putter (left)
compared with one of today's more exotic models*

*Burnham professionals' drivers
David Haines' (left) and Ernie Foord's*

Club-making and repairing was an important element in a pro's income, in an arrangement with his parent club which, at Burnham as everywhere else, was a strange hybrid between master-servant and franchisee. The club would pay the pro a weekly retainer, usually of £1, in return for which he would be expected to set the tees and pin positions, act as starter, man the pro shop and, more often than not, work on the course. Giving lessons and making and repairing clubs were also part of the pro's duties, of course, but he could keep the income from these activities for himself. Ernie charged two shillings and sixpence (about £12.50 in today's money) for an hour's lesson, a figure which the Committee reckoned was rather on the high side. A round with the pro would probably have been more, but in many clubs the pro was expected to make up for time spent on the course by working extra hours in the shop.

Only the professional golfing elite could expect to bolster their incomes significantly with tournament prize-money. A paper published in the *Economic History Review* in 2008 includes an estimate of the earnings of the top 19 professionals in the twenty years from 1894 to 1914. Not surprisingly, Harry Vardon, six times Open Champion during that period, emerges as the leading money winner with the princely total of £1,750. That's £210,000 in today's money, or just over £10,000 a year when averaged over the 20 years. Vardon did, of course, have other sources of income. Spalding paid him $5,000 (over £100,000 now) to promote its equipment during an extended tour of the USA in 1900, while exhibition matches and the side bets that usually went with them were another rich source of income. But the big money was very much confined to the likes of Vardon, Taylor, Braid and Ted Ray. The eighth pro on the prizemoney list, Jack White (Open Champion at Sandwich in 1904), had winnings of just £226 over those 20 years. Even though he was probably among the 50 best golfers in Britain, Ernie Foord's prowess on the course made little or no difference to his earning capacity.

Not that he seems to have done too badly in growing both his business and his income. He took on his younger brother Fred as his assistant as soon as Fred left school, Ernest Whitcombe joined the team in 1907 as caddy-master, and when Fred left in 1908 to become pro at Pennard*, on the Gower peninsula, Ernest took his place as Ernie's assistant, before he too flew the Burnham nest to become a fully-fledged pro at Came Down in Dorset in 1910.

We don't know exactly how many assistants and club-makers were employed in Ernie's shop. We do know that the business was a success. By 1913 the club committee was agreeing to pay for new display cabinets to be installed in the pro shop, while in the following year it paid for two new windows to be created 'to give Foord more light, so that he could employ additional helpers'. A pro was expected to be an employer and a manager, as well as being a salesman, a teacher, a craftsman, a supervisor of trainees and apprentices and, of course, a top-class golfer. All this, and Ernie still not 30 years old!

With his retainer from the club, his income from club-making and repairing, some commission from the caddy fees and the money he earned from coaching, Ernie, as a respected professional in a top-rank club, was probably making something like £250 a year in the run-up to the First World War. That would be the equivalent of around £30,000 today, so not exactly a king's ransom but plenty enough for Ernie to be able to afford to get married, start a family and buy his own property in Burnham. It may be, in fact, that he didn't have much choice when it came to the marriage. He and Ada Gard, a local girl, were married in early 1909. Their son Stanley was born that April! Much tut-tutting in the clubhouse bar, no doubt, but if the match did have something of the shotgun about it, that doesn't seem to have affected its happiness or longevity.

By the time of the 1911 census, the Foord family were living in a smart new terraced house in Dunstan Road. The local boy had made good! His mother and father, meanwhile, were still living in Golf Cottage, behind the clubhouse, despite the fact that Walter had

---

*This doesn't seem to have worked out too happily. Fred's contract excused him from working on the course on Sundays, but he was otherwise expected to be there every day except Christmas Day and Good Friday, including being in attendance on Saturday afternoons, Sunday mornings and general holidays. He left after a year, to return to his brother's shop and fill the vacancy left by Ernest Whitcombe!

The 'smart villa' in Dunstan Road to which Ernie and family moved in 1909

retired as head green-keeper the previous year. It may not have been an entirely amicable parting of the ways, occasioned as it had been by the appointment of Major Archdale as 'Links Superintendant' over Walter's head, and given that Walter was only 51 and that his departure was confirmed 'by a written agreement, signed by Foord, to be kept in the Secretary's office' (which sounds remarkably like a present-day 'compromise agreement'). But the Burnham members were not slow to recognize the contribution which Walter had made in his 20 years with the club. A testimonial fund raised £24 – 6/-, the equivalent of almost £3,000 today. Even though Walter and Sarah were obliged to move out of Golf Cottage a year or two later, to make way for Major Archdale, who had been promoted to Club Secretary, they could now live reasonably comfortably for the rest of their lives.

5

That most astonishing round

Whilst at least 18 of the Berrow caddies may have gone on to become professional golfers in those early years, there were plenty who didn't, and caddying was a tough apprenticeship for all of them. Nonetheless, whilst the rewards for carrying the members' increasingly heavy bags may have been modest, they were more than enough to persuade many a family to allow their young lads to leave school at the earliest possible opportunity to earn their keep on the links. This was, of course, true of every golf club, and it was at a time when, like mushrooms in a damp September, new clubs were springing up all over the place. The implications for the education of the caddies, and by extension their prospects in later life, did not pass unnoticed in the higher reaches of the establishment. No less a figure than Henry Hobhouse, MP for East Somerset, a member of the Government's Board of Education and the architect of the 1902 Education Act, took a keen interest in the subject. In April 1910 he wrote to Burnham and Berrow, as he did to every Somerset golf club, asking the club to take measures to advance the 'education, technical and literacy of the caddies employed by the club'. It has to be said that the committee was not overly impressed. The proposal 'bristled with difficulties'. Hobhouse, however, persisted, and by July the committee was organising evening classes for the caddies, a gesture which once again showed that this was a club with a better developed social conscience than most at the time, even if the experiment was soon abandoned.

A truncated education was by no means the only issue that drew public attention to the welfare of boy caddies. Another was the ever increasing size of the bags they were required to shoulder. There was no limit on the number of clubs a golfer could have in his bag in those days, and with club-makers like Ernie Foord only too happy to craft a club for almost every conceivable exigency, caddies young and old increasingly found themselves staggering under what, in 1912, Bernard Darwin described as 'a truly preposterous armoury of clubs'.

As a former caddy himself, Ernie Foord decided that this was a situation that needed to be highlighted if it was ever going to be changed. And the best way of doing that was obviously to show that good golf could be played with just a handful of clubs (when Francis Ouimet beat Vardon and Ray in a play-off to win the US Open at Garden City in 1913 he had just seven clubs in his bag) or even with just one.

We have already noted his proficiency, learned as a caddy, with just a single club. It was one that he shared with all of the Berrow caddies who went on to become professionals, although none of the others took it to quite such a remarkable level. Ernie could play just about any shot with any club: he could sky a driver like a niblick shot; he could hit a golf ball halfway up with his niblick, so that it rocketed away for the best part of 150 yards; he was the master of the push shot into a head-wind – what we would call now a 'stinger' – with almost any club; and he could lay bunker shot after bunker shot stone dead with his cleek.

But it was with a putter in his hand that Ernie Foord was sans pareil. Off the tee, playing it like a one iron, he could fire the ball well over 200 yards along the flatter fairways, like the new 7th, 8th, 11th and 18th. If there was a giant sandhill in the way, as there was at all of the short holes except the new 13th, he would open the face and hit hard down on the ball, so that it soared from the club as if he were using a mashie, while around the green he had always been deadly. Yes, Ernie Foord could drive a long ball, but it was his putting that set him apart. As JH Taylor was wont to remark, if Harry Vardon putted like Ernie Foord he could never be beaten.

Ah, but what about Burnham's notorious bunkers, you may ask? How did Ernie extricate himself from those? Well, it wasn't a case of him using a cleek-style putter with a few degrees of loft. 'Lynx' in the *Bristol Times and Mirror* is crystal clear on that:

> The putter Foord uses is an ordinary straight-faced weapon, and not, as you would suppose, one with the loft of a putting cleek.

That being so, there was no way that Ernie could escape from Burnham's many steep-faced sandy wastes with anything resembling a conventional bunker shot. He had learned that whilst still in short trousers. Instead, he developed a technique all of his own. He would stand with his back to the direction the ball was intended to go, take the putter in his right hand, swinging it backwards to strike the sand behind the ball with the heel of the club so – hopefully – digging it out. Any golfer who cares to try this method will soon discover that it is not an easy shot to play. The margin for error is non-existent. But having practised it for most of his young life, Ernie was supremely confident about his trademark shot and extremely adept at it.

He was by no means the first golfer to perfect this particular skill. The best-known exponent of putter-only golf was a Mr Charles Hutchings of the Pau club in the south of France. He had once gone round what was admittedly a fairly short and level course in 81, and that was with a gutty, and it was that score that Ernie set himself to beat. On 2 February 1912 he succeeded, going round the 'new' Burnham in 78 shots. But he still felt he could do better. He'd had an expensive tangle with a particularly nasty bunker on the second and had even missed a couple of short putts. Everyone in the club, from the youngest caddy to the most senior member, seemed to be urging him to have another go, and maybe add a world record with his putter to that 'world record' of a 63 back in 1903.

So, on Saturday 16 March he tried again. His partner this time was our old friend Heneage Wheeler, son of the Vicar of Berrow, observant and sympathetic chronicler of village life in Berrow and a more than decent golfer. He played off 8, a figure which rather under-stated his true ability, according to Lynx in the *Bristol Times and Mirror*, and whilst he was obviously keen for Ernie to do well, he was equally determined to give a good account of himself in a match which would be closely followed by just about everyone in the club. Tee-off was arranged for 10 am, after the first batch of members had set off on their medal rounds. It would be played off the medal tees, on a course measuring 6,100 yards, give or take, and Wheeler would start what was a match-play encounter at five up, as well as having the benefit of a full set of clubs. It was a frosty morning, with a biting wind off the sea, a combination which suited Ernie pretty well, given that it added length to his drives as they skittered along the frozen fairways, whilst his putter was the ideal club for keeping the ball down, under the wind. The sun was shining as our two protagonists shook hands on the first tee, in front of a good crowd of members, caddies, family and friends. "Got your caddy then, Ernie?" asked a voice from the crowd to much laughter. Ernie just waved his trusty putter above his head. He had never been one to waste words, and this morning he meant business.

Heneage Wheeler

Mr Wheeler, sir as Ernie called him, had the honour and hit a decent drive which carried the sandhill and finished, out of sight from the tee of course, towards the bottom of the slope beyond, 50 yards or so short of the green. Ernie kept the ball back in his stance and hit down on it hard with his heavy-bladed putter, to send the ball rocketing away like a pheasant, just clearing the top of the hill to finish ten yards beyond his opponent's ball. Wheeler took his light iron from his caddy and played a run up which finished 20 feet or so beyond the flag on the big, saucer-shaped green. Ernie's approach stopped six feet short, but after Wheeler had missed for his three, Ernie made no mistake. The Wheeler lead had been reduced to four.

At 310 yards, the second hole was another shortish two-shotter which needed to be played in two hops, to avoid the nest of craters and bunkers which separated a shallow stretch of fairway from the new green which had recently been created in a hollow just to the right of the previous one. It was thus a lot easier for the amateur with his niblick than for the pro with his putter. Sure enough, Wheeler lofted a well-judged pitch to the middle of the green, while Ernie, anxious above all

Ernie Foord's deadly putter

to make the carry, couldn't quite hold the green, his ball running over the bank at the back. But the one back was simple enough, and he laid it stone dead for a four, and a half, on a dangerous hole.

The third was not so challenging. Played from a tee some 30 yards forward from the modern-day 2nd medal tee, the main priority was to avoid the bunkers right and left which could trap a long drive, after which a straightforward pitch or run-up would find the green, on the flat ground between Majuba and today's 2nd green. Ernie had more than enough power with his putter to send his ball clattering over the ridge in mid-fairway, while there was plenty of room in front of the green to allow him to run his second shot onto it. Wheeler had pushed his drive out to the right, had to hack out from deep rough and could do no better than 5. His lead was down to three. "I'd be better off using your old putter off the tee," he remarked ruefully, as they made their way up the short slope to the 4th tee.

"Well, this is certainly no push-over," responded Ernie, as he surveyed the ridge he would need to carry, with the bridle path beyond it, to reach the safety of the fairway. To the right the sandy wastes of the 16th; to the left a deep, rank, marshy hollow. There was no bail out. He just had to hit as hard as he ever had to power the ball over that sandy ridge and give himself a chance of carrying the deep swale just short of the green with his second. He wasn't a tall man, wasn't Ernie Foord: about five foot nine, slightly built, but wiry, with wrists like steel hawsers. He gave the ball a tremendous crack. It carried the ridge and ran down to the bottom of the slope, to finish on the fairway, some 150 yards short of the green. Wheeler, meanwhile, had again pushed his drive, this time into a horrible sandy lie, leaving him no option but to hack it back into play. Anything better than a five was looking unlikely. But now Ernie faced another big decision. Should he lay up short of the sandy chasm in front of the green and take his chances with a pitch and a putt, or should he go for the carry and risk being buried in the sand? Discretion proved the better part of valour and, as so often, it paid off, a ten-foot putt going down for a par and a win. The deficit was down to two.

But in 1912 as now, disaster is ever lurking just around the next sandhill at Burnham and Berrow. For a golfer armed only with a putter, the 5th hole was a nightmare. At 468 yards it was the longest on the course, from a tee to the right of the 4th green (today's third) to a fairway contoured like a rough sea, the fearsome 'kitchen' to be avoided and then a final pitch over a jumble of humps and hollows to a typical punch-bowl Burnham green in the deep hollow short and right of today's fifth tee. Ernie got his tee shot away all right, but, as so often on this hole, he found it on a steep up slope. To have any chance of reaching the green with his third, he had to clear the kitchen, but therein might lie disaster. Still, with his opponent nicely placed some 50 yards further on, there was nothing for it but to take on the shot. Pressing, he topped it. The ball ran and ran, up hill and down dale, finally coming to rest in – where else? – the kitchen. The ball lay badly, at the front of the bunker. There was only one shot to play, his patent, one-handed, biff with the heel. But if he got it wrong, his hopes of a record might be buried, there and then. Unusually for Ernie, who always played briskly, he stood outside the bunker, rehearsing the shot. "Must keep my head still; must follow through," he was muttering to himself. But when it came to it, the heel of the club thumped into the sand an inch or so further back from the ball than he'd intended. It came out all right, but only a matter of a few yards. So that was three shots, and still a good 150 yards from the green with all sorts of trouble in between. He was staring in the face a seven, perhaps even an eight. But he had a cool head, had Ernie. His opponent was well-placed to pitch onto the green for his five, or possibly even a four, as the ball had a habit of gathering around the pin. The hole was almost certainly gone, but that didn't mean it need ruin his round. So instead of going for a death or glory carry, he calmly rapped his ball 80 or so yards up the fairway, to the edge of the humps and hollows which his fifth would need to carry. If the green played its usual friendly trick, he might still escape with a six. This time he played his shot to perfection, cutting the ball up as high as he could possibly manage, praying all the time that the ball would run all the way up the slope at the back of the green, and then all the way back down, to the pin. So it proved. Wheeler got his five and the win, but Ernie had saved a six and his score. Three down again.

Phew, he thought to himself, as the pair of them climbed up the steep flight of steps to the 6th tee. If I can just get past the next without any serious damage, things will get easier as the fairways get flatter. But getting past the old 6th with just a putter was easier said than done. The tee is more or less the same one as is used for today's short 5th, but the line was away to the right, over the high ridge of sandhills, and so down into another deep punchbowl green this one between today's 13th green and 14th tee. To reach the green, 166 yards away, over that sandy crest with a putter was well-nigh impossible, even for Ernie Foord. He would have to carry the ball as far as he could, hope for some sort of lie and rely on his skill on the green to save not too disastrous a score. And this time the luck was with him. His tee shot carried the ridge and finished halfway down the slope on the other side, mercifully in the clear. Wheeler pulled his cleek shot into the wilderness away to the left. Ernie knew that he just needed to nip his approach nicely. Another gathering green should do the rest. Five minutes later he was walking off with a three, the deficit back to two and with three longer but – crucially – flatter holes to take the pair of them up to the turn.

At the 420-yard 7th (the hole that was the 6th from 1923 to 1978), two fine blows with his putter left him 40 yards short of the green, from where he ran his ball up to eight feet and holed for a par four and another win.

The 8th was another comparatively straightforward hole, over flat ground to a green short and to the right of today's 7th, but well away towards the line of the rhyne (which didn't then exist). There was nothing in the way of two clean straight hits, but over the wettest patch of ground on the entire course in mid-March, the early frostiness rapidly thawing, there wasn't much run for Ernie's putter. It took him three big thumps to reach the green, and this time there was no redeeming single putt. Wheeler also took five to cling onto his slender lead.

It was a similar story at the 9th, another straightaway hole, following the direction of today's 8th but on the drier ground much closer to the sandhills on the right. Wheeler hit a fine drive and a high, floating spoon shot to reach the green in two. Ernie was short in two, but once again his run-up was judged to perfection. A four gave him 37 to the turn, to Wheeler's 42, and just the one hole in it. It was two shots better than his previous best putter-only score to the turn, and he knew that for the homeward journey the wind would be from right to left, becoming more helpful as the finishing line came in sight. "You can do this Ernie," said one of the gaggle of members who were following the match. "You only need to come home in 40 and you'll have beaten your best score."

"We'll see about that," replied Ernie with a wry smile. "There's a few more mountains still to be climbed – starting with this one," he added, pointing his putter at the ridge of sandhills which stood in the way of his next tee shot. "Still," he consoled himself "at least we've got the wind behind."

Burnham's 10th in 1912 measured 220 yards, bogey 4. With the prevailing wind at their backs, the longer hitters could expect to reach what we now know as the 10th green. It had taken its name 'Spion Kop' from the previous 9th and was of a similar length. But, unlike that earlier hole, this version, whilst still a blind hole, at least allowed the golfer to play between the highest of the sandhills, through 'Archdale's Gap' as it was dubbed, rather than having to clear them. It was played from a tee on the ridge above the (now disused) winter tee for today's 9th to a green which was close to today's 10th, with the bunker guarding the left-hand entry to the green. Even though the ground slopes helpfully down towards the green for the last fifty yards or so, it was still what would have been regarded at the time as 'a sporting challenge', especially for a golfer armed with nothing more than a putter!

But Ernie was up for the challenge. He nailed his tee shot, so that it just cleared the furthest ridge of dunes and clattered down the slope beyond to ten yards short of the green. His approach finished three feet away and down went the putt for a win against Wheeler and a gain of a shot on bogey on a tricky hole.

It was the ideal start to the homeward nine and set him up perfectly for the two long holes that lay ahead. The 11th was pretty much the 11th as we have it today, except that the drive was threatened by a bunker up the right at just over 200 yards, rather than on the left. At 400 yards it was out of range in two for Ernie's putter, but the open entrance to the green gave him every chance of running his third up close, which is precisely what he did. Wheeler matched his four with two good shots to the green. Match now all square.

At this point, the course had only very recently been reconfigured. The tee for the 12th was immediately to the west of the 11th green and can still clearly be seen. But instead of being the tee for an undistinguished short hole of 140 yards, it was now being used for the long 12th hole, the Church hole, as the original 12th tee (the same one as is in use today) was regarded as being too close to the Berrow road and to Peregrine Hammond's manor house. At 465 yards, along a narrow fairway between the church and the road to a green beset by elm trees on the church side, it was a bit of a slog and had an almost parkland feel, out of keeping with the rest of the course. It became well known, mainly because it couldn't be played when the church was in use on Sundays and for weddings and funerals at other times, so that a Sunday green had to be created, cut into the sandhill to the left of today's 12th fairway (and recently obliterated by the re-modelling of that hole). But it certainly wasn't Hugh Alison's favourite hole. In his 1925 report on the course, he described it as 'a dull hole for those who cannot reach the green in two, and not very exciting for those who can'. Ernie, with his putter, was most definitely in the former category, but three raking blows took him to the front edge, and two putts from there produced a bogey 5. Wheeler holed a putt for a four, to stop the rot, at least temporarily, in the match.

The 13th was a new short hole, to replace the now abandoned 12th. It was played from a tee above and to the right of the 12th green to another low-lying green, between the slope of the sandhills to the right and rushes on the left. Alison regarded it as a thoroughly bad, fluky hole and recommended its replacement by a new short hole, which would become the 14th, a proposal that was eventually adopted. Ernie had only played this new 13th a couple of times, but he knew enough to hold his tee shot well out to the right, from where it duly trundled down to the edge of the green for a comfortable three.

So that was level fours, with five to play. Ernie was on track to win the match and handsomely beat his own record with the putter. Yet he knew perfectly well that, over Burnham's testing homeward stretch, nothing could be taken for granted, starting with his very next hole, the famous Old Mill hole. This took its name from the remains of a windmill which stood just behind the tee, a windmill which was notorious for a Mrs Hicks having murdered her husband there after he had come home drunk once too often. The tee shot had to carry the high-banked track called the Old Kent Road, and it needed to be nicely judged, as the ideal line was down the right, which brought the track into play, whereas the safer line down the left would leave a long and tricky second shot to the well-bunkered green. Go too far left, and you were out of bounds. Ernie had thought long and hard about this particular shot. A pulled tee shot would make life difficult; a slice would be disastrous. This thought was in his mind, even as he swung. Sure enough, his wrists turned ever so slightly as he struck the ball, producing a snap hook which was within an ace of being what the older members called a 'founder'. The ball carried the track – just – but finished in thick rough to the left of the fairway, just a few feet from the out-of-bounds hedge. Heneage Wheeler, who was as keen as anyone to see Ernie break his record, came over to have a look and made the sort of sound that plumbers do when confronted with a broken-down dish-washer.

What now? If Ernie tried a conventional shot, using the putter as if it were a long iron, it might get tangled in the grass and barely move the ball at all. And there was certainly no loft to work with so as to be able to chop it out. There was only one thing for it – his signature shot, that patent, one-handed backhand shot that he used to get out of bunkers. It was a shot that he had taught himself as a boy, playing one-club golf against the Whitcombes on their improvised course, and it was his only hope. So he turned his back on the intended direction of travel, grasped the club firmly in his right hand, tilted his head to the right so that he could see the ball, took a deep breath and swung. And, heaven be praised, it worked! The heel of the club cut through the thick nest of grass and struck the ball perfectly, on a rising arc, to impart the necessary top-spin. The ball shot out, not so much like a scalded cat as a startled weasel, finishing safely in the fairway some 30 yards further on. "Great shot, Ern," shouted the boy caddies who had come to cheer their hero down the home stretch. "Well played, Foord," pronounced the club President, Monsignor Kennard, who had come out to join the party in the hope of witnessing golfing history. Ernie smiled and wiped some imaginary sweat from his brow. The crisis was past, for now.

But there was still work to be done. He needed two more blows to reach the front edge of the green, and two putts from there meant a six. The only consolation was that Wheeler had tangled unhappily with the Old Kent Road and taken seven, to be one down again.

So to the 15th, which was very much the same hole as today's, as played from the winter tee about 100 yards ahead of the championship tee. There was no question of carrying the ridge, so Ernie played safely out to the right, hit his second to about 60 yards short of the green and then played a perfect approach, using the contours on the right-hand side of the green to guide the ball to within a few feet of the back-left pin. Down for four, one better than Wheeler, who was now two down.

The 16th was another hole which would immediately be recognisable to today's Burnham golfer, with one significant difference. Instead of just the one bunker threatening the drive down the right, there was then a stretch of sandy rough, the nastiest part of which was 'Hutchinson's bunker'. So the key to the hole, even more then than now, was to keep the drive well out to the left. The fairway was rather wet and heavy after the thaw, so that Ernie's tee shot pulled up fully 120 yards short of the green. But he fairly drilled his second to the front edge, whereupon he calmly rolled his approach putt up over the bank – and into the hole for a three! Wheeler's steady four wasn't enough, and that was that as far as the match was concerned: Ernest Foord the victor, 3/2. The two men doffed their caps and shook hands, as a steadily growing crowd applauded. "Brilliant, Foord, just brilliant," said Heneage Wheeler. "Just make sure you don't mess it up here, at Majuba."

Majuba, as we have seen, was the name that had been given to the towering conical sandhill, on which – its peak now lopped off – the tees for the 3rd and 17th (medal) are now situated. It was originally played east to west from a tee well away to the left of the present 16th green, to a green on the far side of the hill, 25 yards or so short of today's 2nd green. The 1901 course changes saw it re-orientated onto more of a north-south line, but to the same green as previously, bunkered on either hand, to the left of the present day blue tee at the 17th. It was 204 yards long and played every inch of it, given the elevation needed on the tee shot to clear Majuba's daunting pinnacle. Elevation was something that Ernie Foord, armed only with his putter, could not command. But there was no realistic way around Majuba, so nothing to be done except hit and hope maybe for a skip over the top and a helpful bounce or two down the far side.

As soon as he hit his shot, Ernie knew that he hadn't made the carry. His ball lay on the upslope, some 20 feet from the summit, but it was at least lying cleanly on the sand. It meant another completely blind shot but, with the upslope to help him, he should at least be able to get the ball in the air. He played the shot well enough, but his ball ran through the green and over the back. His approach putt from there was close, but not close enough. So that was a four, albeit on a bogey four hole, but it still felt like a shot dropped.

And so to the last, the hole which Herbert Fowler had designed and very much the same 18th as today, requiring a long, right-to-left tee shot and then a wood or long iron for the second, depending on the wind. But there was this important difference back then. The line of sandhills 100 yards or so short of the green which was cut through at Harry Colt's instigation in the 1920s then stretched uninterruptedly across the line of the second shot, offering the player no sight of the green. Fortunately the wind was in Ernie's favour. His tee shot finished more than 200 yards down the fairway. Yet again he faced a dilemma. Should he go for the carry and risk getting tangled up in the tufty sedges on the sandy ridge, or play safe and leave his second shot sufficiently far back to be able to clear the obstacle with his third and trust to a single putt? After reaching the turn in 37 and surviving that crisis at the 13th, he had set his heart on a 72 and level fours. To have any hope of the three he needed he would have to attempt the carry. He hit the ball perfectly. The shot was so well timed that he barely felt the impact through his fingers. Surely the ball would carry the ridge and run on down to the green. But no. Agonisingly it just clipped the very top of the ridge, to finish halfway down the further slope. "What bad luck," commiserated Heneage Wheeler, as a collective groan went up from the crowd, now some fifty strong. "Oh well," replied Ernie, "let's see if we can get down in a couple more, for a 73."

He clipped his third sweetly. As so often on that 18th green, the ball nodded at the hole before finishing 25 feet past. Ernie reckoned that his putt for a four would break maybe six inches left, and he knew it would need to be hit firmly, up the green and into the breeze, but not so firmly as to leave him four or five feet coming back. The crowd fell silent as he addressed the ball, using the palm grip which had served him so well. He'd picked the line, he knew the speed and he had holed hundreds of putts like this on Burnham greens over the past 12 years. He produced his usual slow, smooth stroke.

The crowd held their breath … the ball was on line … the pace was good … could it? … might it? ……… It's in!

What a roar went up, as first Heneage Wheeler, then Monsignor Kennard and then Archdale came up to shake Ernie warmly by the hand. All the Foord family were there, his mother and father, Sarah and Walter, his brothers Fred and Bill and, most important of all, his wife Ada, holding little Stan in her arms. There were no hugs and kisses. That would never do in full view of the clubhouse, surrounded by all those gentlemen golfers. But Ernie's mum just couldn't resist giving him a peck on the cheek, while Ada squeezed his hand in a way that spoke volumes and simply beamed with pride.

As for Ernie himself, he initially just stood there, as his ball disappeared into that final hole, looking almost bemused as the cheers rang round the 18th green. But then his broad features broke into a trade-mark grin. He'd done it: 73 around Burnham off the medal tees with just a putter. It was surely a record that would never be broken, his guarantee of golfing immortality.

"Allow me to buy you a celebratory drink in the clubhouse," said Heneage Wheeler, with typical generosity. "That's very kind of you, Mr Wheeler, sir, but I've promised Mr Akerman I'd have his light iron re-shafted by this evening, and I'd really better see to that."

But Ernie, Walter, Bill and Fred drank plenty of Tom Holt's beer in the Berrow Inn that night!

David Haines recreating the putt at the 18th that Ernie Foord holed for his 73

73 with a putter

Burnham & Berrow Golf Club
16 March 1912
Ernie Foord (one putter) v Heneage Wheeler (a bag of clubs)
Wheeler starting 5 up

hole	yards	bogey	Foord	Wheeler	Match score
1	232	4	3	4	W+4
2	310	4	4	4	W+4
3	350	4	4	5	W+3
4	368	5	4	5	W+2
5	468	5	6	5	W+3
6	166	3	3	5	W+2
7	420	5	4	5	W+1
8	410	5	5	5	W+1
9	397	5	4	4	W+1
	3121	40	37	42	
10	220	4	3	4	A/S
11	400	5	4	4	A/S
12	465	5	5	4	W+1
13	145	3	3	4	A/S
14	404	5	6	7	F+1
15	367	5	4	6	F+2
16	327	4	3	4	Foord wins 3/2
17	204	4	4	3	
18	440	5	4	5	
	2972	40	36	41	
	6093	**80**	**73**	**83**	

Word of Ernie's well-nigh miraculous achievement soon spread. It was the main subject of the 'Golfing Notes' by 'Lynx' in the following Saturday's *Bristol Times and Mirror*. Under the headline FOORD'S UNCANNY PUTTER, he wrote:

> Ernest Foord's latest performance with a putter only, of giving an 8-handicapped man, a player under-handicapped rather than over, 5 up and a beating by 3/2 is illustration that it is possible to play good golf without the assistance of 10 or 12 clubs. The Burnham professional holed-out the course in 73 strokes – five strokes better than on a previous occasion this year, when he essayed a similar task.
>
> This was a remarkable performance, especially so seeing that the putter Foord uses is an ordinary straight-faced weapon and not, as one would suppose, one with the loft of a putting cleek.

A week later, and news had reached the golf correspondent of *The Times* and much the most respected writer about the game of his or any other era, Bernard Darwin:

> The news of a remarkable golfing achievement has lately come from Burnham in Somersetshire.
>
> Ernest Foord, the professional, armed only with a putter, gave a start of 5 holes to an 8 handicap player and beat him by three holes up with two to play, completing the round in a score of 73 strokes.
>
> This is a truly astonishing score, because Burnham is neither a particularly short nor a particularly easy course. A year or two ago, when the game consisted largely of hitting the ball over a link* and then running to the top to see what had happened on the green on the far side, there was always the chance that good golf and good fortune combined would produce a miraculously low score. Those who love blind shots will never again be able to enjoy such a crowded two

---

* *OED: Link: rising ground, ridge or bank.*

> hours (!) of glorious life as they could on the old unregenerate Burnham, but in its place they have now got a really fine course with plenty of length and difficulty, and just enough mountaineering to give a spice to life. Moreover, since the sandhills of Burnham are veritable "sky-scrapers" of their kind, it would not, prima facie, seem to be a course well adapted to the putter, a club naturally of pedestrian and "scuffling" proclivities.

Darwin goes on to express some scepticism as to the description of Ernie's putter as 'straight-faced', attributing what he called 'this hyperbole' to the enthusiasm of the moment. And he was probably correct in suggesting that, of the putters of that era, 'but few are quite straight-faced, and those few are usually to be found in the bags of the worst and not the best of players.'

As for the lesson to be drawn from Ernie's achievement, to Darwin, it was this:

> That it is in learning the game rather than in playing it that there is much virtue in few clubs. The professional in the early days of his caddie-hood has an extremely small stock of clubs: he will be a lucky boy if he has more than one ... So, with necessity to drive him he learns to play a variety of strokes with one and the same club. He learns that if his single iron will hit the ball too far with a full shot, he just has to play a half shot; that the ball by some method or other must be kept down against a wind and must be heavily cut if it is to pitch dead over a bunker. He and his club master these difficulties together and become part of one another in a way rarely to be found amongst amateurs.

Well, Ernie and his putter were certainly part of one another on that March Saturday in 1912, and what a shame it is that the weapon which repaid his skill so well seems subsequently to have been lost.

6

Last years at Burnham

His miraculous round with the putter and the brief sunburst of celebrity that went with it did not change Ernie Foord's life. That autumn he reached the quarter finals of the News of the World for the second time, at a very wet Sunningdale, and after two good wins found himself up against his fellow West Countryman and renowned club-maker, Harry Cawsey, born at Westward Ho! but professional by this stage at Seacroft in Lincolnshire. It was not a great match – neither Cawsey nor Foord played anything more than ordinary golf,' pronounced Bernard Darwin – with Cawsey going through by 2/1, only to be then crushed by the awesome power of Ted Ray. Harry Vardon won a famous final on the last green. Ernie Foord went home £15 the richer. That's £1,700 or so in today's money, so it was not an entirely fruitless expedition.

Back at Burnham, there had been changes in the staffing, following on from the completion of the handsome new clubhouse, built in 1910, at a cost of £1,450 (which, at £166,000 after allowing for inflation sounds like remarkably good value for money). Major Archdale was promoted from Course Superintendant to paid Secretary, at a salary of £36 a year, Tom Holt remaining as Honorary Secretary, and the committee had decided that they were no longer satisfied with 'women servants' and wanted instead a 'Mess Sergeant'. The services of Sarah Foord and Bessie Whitcombe were accordingly dispensed with, a new steward and his wife taking over. However, Sarah and Walter were still living in Golf Cottage (putting up with persistent problems with the drains), so occupying a property which the committee understandably thought would be better occupied by a club employee. Their initial thought was that Ernie should live there, rather than in town, so that he could be on hand whenever needed by the membership, and his mother and father were therefore given notice.

But, as we have already seen, the Foord family did not take kindly to being pushed around at the whim of the club's grandees. Ernie dug in his heels and refused to move, conscious that by now the club needed him more than he needed the club, while Walter and Sarah stayed put, at least until the summer of 1912, when they moved out to a home of their own, and Major Archdale moved in.

Apart from the Open and the News of World and its regional qualifiers, the only really competitive golf played by professionals was challenge matches. Ernie played plenty of these, usually to mark the opening of a new course, or an extension from nine to 18 holes. But the really big draws were the Triumvirate – Vardon, Taylor and Braid. A match between two of those great men could be guaranteed to draw the crowds and raise the profile; better still if someone like Sandy Herd or Ted Ray could be persuaded to make up a foursome, as in the famous match.

As the club's first professional, JH Taylor had a natural affinity with Burnham and Berrow. He had played Andrew Kirkaldy there in 1892, beaten James Braid when the course was extended to 18 holes in 1897, celebrated the 1901 extension with a 36-hole match against Vardon (not actually played until 1903), and it was Braid again whom he faced in 1910 to inaugurate the Herbert Fowler improvements to the course. But Taylor was also happy to take on Ernie Foord, having known him since he was a scruffy seven-year-old, knocking a ball around with a cut-down cleek. They played twice: that 1901 encounter already described, in which Ernie was rather overcome with nerves, and a contest twelve years later.

The second match was arranged for 27 September 1913. JH Taylor was on something of a tour of the West Country, having played at Weston-super-Mare the previous day. It was a typically windy Burnham day, with a strong breeze off the sea which, as so often, got stronger as the day went on. JH was not at his best, having been 'not well for some time past'. When the *Bristol Times and Mirror*'s golf correspondent, 'Lynx', asked him whether he felt he could rise to the occasion, he replied, with typical humour, that he doubted it "because I haven't a jump in me"!

Sure enough, he started slowly, to be out in 42 and four down to Ernie. There was nothing wrong with his driving or his play with the brassie or the cleek, we are told, but for once his skill with the mashie deserted him, and the putts refused to drop. The deficit soon became five, as Taylor made a mess of the 10th to take six on what was really no more than a long par 3. But from the 11th onwards, the champion's golf regained its customary accuracy. He played the last eight holes in 31 and, with the wind behind, both golfers hit what Lynx described as 'some tremendously long shots'. Ernie was equal to the challenge, however. He missed the green at the short 13th to lose that, but otherwise matched his distinguished opponent shot for shot, hole for hole, to go into lunch 4 up.

The wind was even stronger in the afternoon, and the golf better, even if, according to Lnyx's critical eye, it was still 'far from perfect'. Taylor showed exactly what was meant by that when he reduced the deficit to three with a good up-and-down for a three at the first, only to three-putt the next two for halves at holes he should have won. Ernie restored his four-hole lead when Taylor took four at the 6th, and it was still four at the turn. But then came the Taylor charge which Ernie knew was coming. Flu or no flu, JH's fighting spirit rose within him as they turned for home. He started back 3, 4, 4, 3, to Ernie's 4, 4, 5, 4, to close the gap to just one with five to play. It would have been all square, had Taylor not missed from six feet for his 3 at the 11th, after a glorious cleek shot.

Few in the big crowd doubted that the writing was on the wall. Instead, it was Foord who forged ahead, as Taylor missed short putts at 14 and 15 to lose both. The 16th was halved in fours, and when Ernie holed a good putt at Majuba it was all over. There must have been mixed feelings among the spectators, for JH was still a Burnham hero. But to see their very own 'Berrow caddie' defeat one of the three greatest golfers in the world was a great moment, and no one was happier and more generous in his praise than JH Taylor himself.

And that was it for Ernie Foord as far as 'big golf' in Britain was concerned. He didn't play in the Open in the following year, and in August the outbreak of war with Germany turned everyone's world upside down. Not immediately, it should be said. For a time, life at Burnham went on much as usual. But when Tom Holt's son Cecil was killed in action in September, the war suddenly seemed horribly close. Harry Colt's ambitious plans for re-modelling the course, first discussed in 1913, were put on hold, and the green staff thinned out to a bare minimum, as more and more of the younger members left to join the fight. The club still ticked over, but little more than routine maintenance was carried out on the course, and some of the less sandy areas were turned over to growing hay and vegetables for the war effort. As membership declined and visitor numbers shrank, so economies became inevitable. The club had taken on a hefty overdraft when it built the clubhouse and bought the land around it, and by January 1916 the overdraft had reached the equivalent in today's money of over £100,000. Ernie and three other members of staff volunteered a cut in their wages, but even that was not enough. In January the Committee decided to ask Ernie to get himself a job for the remainder of the war. They would keep his position open for him but in the meantime would manage without a full-time pro.

We have no reason to believe that Ernie Foord was anything other than patriotic, but conscription was looming and he had a wife and young son to support. He had met and befriended several of the young American golfers at various Opens and they had always said to him that if ever he fancied a change from Burnham's sand, worms and winds, the opportunities across the Atlantic for a golfer, teacher and club-maker of Ernie's quality were virtually limitless. He and Ada decided together that it was time to take advantage of those contacts and to seek their fortune in the USA, if not for ever, then certainly for the duration of the war.

On 5 April the Committee's Chairman reported 'that the Professional Ernest Foord was sailing for America on Saturday April 8.' The minute book goes on to record that 'he spoke about the length of his services to the Club, and his qualities as a man and as a club maker, and proposed that a letter embodying the appreciation in which he is held by the club, which he read to the Committee, be signed by himself, chairman of the committee, and the Hon Sec, and presented to him.'

And that was the end of Ernie Foord's association with Burnham and Berrow Golf Club. One of Ernie's assistants, a G Rawlings, was asked to take over at a salary of 10/- per week (less than half of what Ernie would have been paid, pre-war), plus 9d in every 2/6 for lessons and rounds, plus the privilege to claim old balls not claimed within a reasonable period of time. But it wasn't long before Rawlings was called up and, in a clear sign of what wartime had done to the club, the 15-year-old son of a Mrs Luscombe was trained up to repair clubs.

In leaving, Ernie offered the club the entire contents of his shop for £64 (£5,600), which must have been a fair offer, as it was unanimously accepted by the committee. They were also as good as their word in keeping Ernie's position open for him, should he wish to return. In February 1919 the Assistant Secretary reported that he had written to Ernest Foord three weeks or a month previously, asking whether he intended to return but had received no reply. Conscious that they could hardly be without a full-time professional now that the war was over and the club was rapidly recovering, the committee felt that they had no option but to write to him again, saying that as he hadn't answered their first letter, they had gone ahead and filled his place.

Unsurprisingly Ernest Whitcombe was their first choice, but he turned them down, citing 'the many difficulties in the way' including the insuperable problem of finding a house for himself and his family. So, instead, they decided to approach another one-time Berrow caddie, but this one a bachelor and so less concerned about the accommodation issue: Bob Bradbeer, so inaugurating a Bradbeer dynasty which would endure for a further 60 years. You could say that this was Ernie Foord's parting gift.

7

Ernie (and Fred) in America

Ernie, Ada and little Stan sailed for New York from Liverpool on Saturday 8 April 1916, full of hope, anticipation and, among the adults, some trepidation. Everyone on board was acutely conscious that a German U-boat had sunk the Lusitania off the coast of Ireland less than a year previously, with the loss of over a thousand passengers and crew. They probably travelled second class, at a cost of around £15 per head, or around £1,000 at present day values, so it was a huge investment in the future. Even though Ernie knew that he had a job waiting for him, he was effectively betting his life savings on the move being a success.

From New York the family embarked on a train journey of over 1,000 miles to Kansas City, where Ernie was to take up a post as professional at the recently redesigned Hillcrest Golf Club. Why Hillcrest? The honest answer is that, in the absence (to date) of any Foord family records, we don't know. However, one possibility is that it sprang from the fraternity of golf architects. The new Hillcrest layout had been designed by Donald Ross, the Scotsman from Dornoch who was already one of the most famous American golf architects, thanks to his work at Pinehurst and elsewhere. It is more than possible that he had been tipped the wink by his fellow architect, Herbert Fowler of Walton Heath fame, who knew all about the qualities and abilities of the Foord brothers from his time at Burnham.

Not that they were 'Foord' brothers any more. Ernie had presumably decided that 'Foord' had a slightly pretentious ring to it and it was a bore having to spell it out whenever he was asked his name. So plain and simple 'Ford' he became, with Fred following suit when he joined his brother in Kansas City in January 1920, after a spell at St Enodoc in Cornwall, having presumably avoided being called up for war service because of the ill-health which plagued his later years.

Their arrival in the US could hardly have been better timed. A golf boom was in progress, on the back of Francis Ouimet's remarkable triumph in the 1913 US Open at Brookline, when he beat the British giants, Harry Vardon and Ted Ray, in a play-off. And nowhere was golf booming more spectacularly than in the Mid-West. The effects of the war in Europe had yet to be felt, and new golf courses were being opened or extended with every year that passed. The opportunities for a golf professional who was well-organised, hard-working and could play a bit were almost limitless, especially if he was, like Ernie and Fred, an accomplished club-maker and renowned teacher, given the demand there was for equipment and instruction from all the new starters in the game.

Fred Foord had always been a bit more of a gadfly than Ernie, plying his trade at Pennard, South Wales' 'links in the sky' and as an assistant to James Braid at Walton Heath, as well as his spells at Burnham and St Enodoc. He may even have travelled to Canada in 1913 to become the Royal Regina GC's first professional, assuming he is the 'Fred Ford from Scotland who laid out the five Western holes' referred to in the club's history.

Judging from the few photographs that have survived, he was a stockier, more jowly man than his brother. And if he never matched Ernie's most remarkable feats – that course record 63 at Burnham or the 73 with the putter – he must have been very nearly as good a player and almost as well known in the US. His first job when he arrived in the US in January 1920 was as professional at the Lakewood Golf and Country Club, charged with getting what was a new course ready for play that April. Lakewood was just up the road from Meadow Lake, where Ernie was working, and the pair of them soon moved on to better jobs, Ernie at Plum Hollow and Fred at the Kansas City Golf and Country Club.

Despite their new responsibilities, they still found plenty of time to compete, either individually or as a well-nigh unbeatable team in foursomes. While he was at Hillcrest, Ernie had set the course record with a 70, and he did the same at Meadow Lake (71), St Joseph Country Club (65) and Mission Hills in 1920, also with a 65, which must have been a terrific round on one of the toughest courses in the state.

But it was as a pair that the brothers made their biggest mark on US golf. In 1920, their reputation as match players already established, they were given the honour of being the first opponents of Harry Vardon and Ted Ray, in their seven-week, 41-match tour of the USA. They played the match over 36 holes at Fred's home course of Lakewood, the Fords winning comfortably enough. Two further famous victories followed in 1921, against the young British tigers George Duncan and Abe Mitchell and, perhaps most remarkably of all, against the reigning Open Champion, Jock Hutchinson, and the US Open Champion, Jim Barnes. All of these contests were over 36 holes at Kansas City and, being exhibition matches, were played as fourballs, as opposed to foursomes, which were never a particularly favoured format on that side of the Atlantic. No doubt modest wagers would have been involved, which would have done the Ford finances no harm at all!

In 1921 Ernie took a break from golf and sailed back to England, perhaps for the funeral of either his mother or father and to renew old acquaintances at Burnham, where he was received not quite as a conquering hero but certainly as a local boy who had made very good. He even found time for a round or two of golf with young Bob Bradbeer whom he had known so well when they were both growing up in Berrow. And he must have been hugely impressed with the new holes which had been built under the guidance of Harry Colt and Hugh Alison, even if they had only very recently come into play.

Colt and Alison. They rank alongside the likes of Alister MacKenzie, Donald Ross, Pete Dye and AW Tillinghast as the best and most prolific golf course architects in the game's history. And at the very same time that Ernie Ford was enjoying the fruits of their labours at Burnham, they were hard at work laying out a brand new course at Plum Hollow in Southfield, Michigan, just north-west of Detroit. The fact that Alison and Colt were hired to construct what was right from the start intended to be one of the finest courses in the state says all that is needed about the ambitions of Plum Hollow's founders, and they were determined to hire a professional of the quality to match that of their new course.

So Plum Hollow's President, Arthur J Hood, turned to Michigan's most successful golf professional, Leo Diegel, for advice. Diegel – who added the word 'diegeling' to the golfing lexicon on account of his ungainly but remarkably successful elbows-out putting style – had twice been Michigan champion and knew all the pros on what was still at the time a fairly limited circuit. He had played with and against the Ford brothers and, besides admiring their golfing-abilities, he had heard all about Ernie Ford's club-making and teaching skills. Ernie had probably learned of the new venture through the Colt-Alison connection, and when Diegel asked him if he was interested, he jumped at the chance.

'PLUM HOLLOW CLUB LANDS STAR 'PRO' IN ERNEST FORD' read the headline in the *Detroit Times*, when Ernie's appointment was announced in early 1922.

Plum Hollow, where Ernie Foord was the professional from 1922 to 1924

'Although he has participated in none of the big competitions on this side, Ford nevertheless has established himself as a splendid golfer,' the article continued, before adding by way of further explanation for what must have been something of a surprise choice: 'More is required of a professional than that he be a good player. He must, among other things, be a good club-maker and teacher. Ford meets these requirements and has been recommended to Plum Hollow as one of the best club-makers in the game.'

No doubt encouraged by his new employers Ernie did make a rare tournament appearance in September that year, in the Western Open which was played just up the road at Oakland Hills. It was won by the Oakland Hills professional, Mike Brady, who had twice been beaten in a play-off for the US Open, of whom more anon. Ernie finished a respectable joint 17th, doing enough both on and off the course to make his mark with the club's elders, as subsequent events would demonstrate.

The brothers must have been fairly close, as when Ernie moved from Kansas to Detroit in early 1922 to take up his position at Plum Hollow, Fred was following in his footsteps barely nine months later, when he was appointed as professional at the Red Run GC, a high-end private members' club at Royal Oak, just a few miles from Plum Hollow. In the meantime he had made the first of his two appearances in the US Open, competing at Skokie that July. He qualified comfortably for the final two rounds and finished in a tie for 47th, his score of 315 leaving him 27 shots adrift of Gene Sarazen, who edged out Bobby Jones in a dramatic final round to win his first major Championship.

Golf was a distinctly seasonal activity in Michigan in the 1920s, with the courses snowbound for most of the winter months. So, enterprising businessman that he evidently was, Fred had established an indoor school in Detroit which kept him busy and no doubt provided a useful income from November through to the beginning of March. He had done much the same when he was in Kansas City, making a deal with the Rothschild's department store to provide winter lessons along with the Scottish professional, Tom Clark.

8

Oakland Hills

The founders of the Oakland Hills Country Club made no bones about their ambition to create one of the most prestigious clubs and courses in the USA. The prime movers were two senior executives of the Ford Motor Company: Joseph Mack, in charge of advertising, and Norval Hawkins, the chief accountant. In October 1916 they brought together 47 of their friends and Detroit business associates at the Detroit Athletic Club to set the wheels in motion, with the annual subscription being fixed at $250 – over £5,000 at today's prices! It was a world away, and not only geographically, from that meeting in Bridgwater in 1890 when Burnham and Berrow GC had been formed.

Finance having been secured, the founders bought 250 acres of farmland, 170 acres being ear-marked for the course and the remaining 80 acres for luxury housing, so setting a pattern which has been followed on thousands of occasions subsequently. In keeping with their high ambitions, they hired one of the most renowned golf architects of the day, Donald Ross, a Scotsman of humble origins in Dornoch, who had emigrated to the States in 1900, graduated from professional golfer to course architect and made an international name for himself with designs like the incomparable Pinehurst No. 2.

Ross took one look at the stretch of land in question and, like Canon Kennard before him at Burnham, pronounced that it was heaven-sent to become a golf course. Work started in earnest on what would become the South Course the following year, with a grand opening taking place in July 1918. As for a professional, the founders decided that they need look no further than arguably one of the best golfers in the country, and certainly the most flamboyant, Walter Hagen. Hagen had won the US Open in 1914 and the Western Open in 1916 and never entertained the slightest doubt as to his own abilities.

"Waal, who's going to be second?" he would invariably drawl on arriving for a tournament, and his record of 11 major championships and 45 US PGA wins more than justified his tongue-in-cheek boastfulness.

'The Haig', as he was known, did not come cheap. He was hired by Joe Mack on a retainer of $300 a month, plus any profit on the sale of golf equipment. That's the equivalent of £5,700 a month in today's money – a king's ransom by the standards of what a golf pro could have expected to earn in 1917. At Burnham Ernie Foord had been more than content with £250 a year.

Hagen enjoyed his time at Oakland Hills and in particular the fact that he was treated as he felt he ought to be treated, not just as a star golfer but as a social equal with the club's membership, no matter how high and mighty – and wealthy – they might be. He was a great favourite with the members both on and off the course – especially in the clubhouse bar, where he would hold court for hours on end. He stayed for three years before deciding that the life of a club professional was not for him and becoming the first pro to make his living from tournaments and his many business ventures, unattached to any club.

Hagen signed off his time at Oakland Hills in typical style – by winning the US Open at Brae Burn in an 18 holes play-off, having been up all night the night before, partying with Al Jolson. The man he beat by a single shot in that play-off was Mike Brady, who only weeks later succeeded him at Oakland Hills. Brady was another one who was a tournament golfer first and a club pro second, and when he decided, in 1924, that it was time to move on – to become Winged Foot in New York State's first professional – the club decided on a change of policy.

For their new pro, Oakland Hills' President Joe Mack would be looking for someone who was both a top golfer and would have the time and inclination to devote most of his time to teaching, club-making and running the professional's shop. So although such a plum job aroused huge interest among the US golf professional fraternity – speculation as to who might get it included 'almost every professional from Jim Barnes to Felix Umph from the Unkept Golf and Country Club', speculated the *Detroit Free Press*, picturesquely – it was unsung Ernie Ford who took the prize.

'A distinct surprise,' commented the *Free Press*'s golf correspondent, FW Drunkenbrod, rather sniffily. 'Whilst he is a good golfer, ranking among the scratch men of the Detroit district, Ernie Ford never has gone in strongly for tournament golf,' he added. 'He is a capable instructor *(more faint praise)* and he has gained no little distinction as a club maker. This, rather than his abilities as a player, won him the Oakland Hills position.'

But if FW Drunkenbrod was unimpressed by the selection, that wasn't the view taken in the boardrooms of Plum Hollow and Oakland Hills. No sooner had his appointment been announced than Ernie found himself at the centre of a bitter battle between the two clubs. On the morning of 9 February 1924, he found himself being claimed as their professional by both of them! It appeared that Plum Hollow had offered Ernie a new contract, for 1924, the previous October. He hadn't signed it because – the family assertiveness greatly to the fore – he didn't think the terms were generous enough. So when Oakland Hills came calling, he felt free to go. But what he had done, as Plum Hollow's President was quick to assert, was to accept three monthly 'checks' for his services, which, he argued, amounted to de facto acceptance. So Ernie Ford was still Plum Hollow's man.

Neither Ernie nor his new employers were having any of it. The contract had been explicitly rejected, and Ernie wasted no time in penning a letter of resignation, enclosing 'checks' of his own to cover the three payments. Aha, came back Plum Hollow, how can he resign from a contract which he said he'd rejected? He's still ours.

Oakland Hills stood firmly behind their new pro, and the unseemly wrangle ended up being referred to something called the Detroit District Golf Association, which didn't have the power to do anything but to offer its advice. So Oakland Hills got their man, and Ernie had the satisfaction of being fought over by two of the smartest clubs in the Mid-West.

While Ernie Ford couldn't command the sort of salary that Hagen was paid, he was by now very comfortably off. We don't know where he and Ada had set up home in Detroit, but it wouldn't be in the least bit surprising if they had bought one of Joe Mack's new houses next to the golf club or at the very least been given the use of one to live in. Their son Stanley, now 15, was growing up into a more than useful golfer, before joining Ernie's staff as an assistant and going on to become a fully-fledged professional in his own right. He and Fred Ford's son Jerry tied equal third in a tournament at Lochmoor and Detroit Country Club in 1929, Jerry winning a special prize – put up by his father!

Life must have seemed very sweet for Somerset's unsung hero of golf, and there was even better to come.

That summer of 1924, Oakland Hills was due to host the US Open on its championship South Course (work on the slightly less exacting North course, intended mainly for the members, was just getting under way). All of the big US names would be there: the defending champion Bobby Jones, Tommy Armour, Wild Bill Mehlhorn, Gene Sarazen, Chick Evans, Macdonald Smith and Walter Hagen, of course. Disappointingly as far as Ernie was concerned, there was no British invasion to try to capture the USA's greatest golfing prize. There were the ex-pats, like Jim Barnes from Lelant and Tommy Armour and Mac Smith from Scotland, but they had long since come to be regarded as Americans, so that only a handful of players entered under anything but the Stars and Stripes: Bobby Cruickshank, beaten in a play off by Jones the previous year, Willie Ogg for Scotland and a largely unknown English pro called Cyril Walker from Manchester by way of the several unremarkable US clubs where he'd worked since emigrating in 1914. Ernie Ford must have been immensely proud as the host professional.

The course was long, difficult and very windy. In the *Detroit Free Press*, our old friend FW Drunkenbrod was making much of the fact that even the big hitters would need to use wooden clubs, spoons or even brassies, to reach the long par 4s in two shots. Of all the players in the field, Cyril Walker seemed just about the least likely to measure up to the task. Standing just five feet six inches tall, no more than nine stone in weight, with crooked teeth, sticky-out ears and a reputation for being rather over-fond of a drink, he looked every inch the 100 to 1 outsider he was. But Cyril had a cussed streak. He was known as the slowest pro in the business, regularly having to be chivvied along by the officials and irritating his playing partners so much that he was often sent out on his own, with just a marker, at the tail of the field. But on this occasion he had prepared well, he had his wife with him to make sure he didn't over-indulge and, having grown up as a golfer on the windswept links of Hoylake, he knew how to keep his ball down through the wind.

His first three rounds were steadiness itself – 74, 74, 74 – to be level with Bobby Jones, three shots up on Cruickshank and with four in hand on Hagen. They played 36 holes on the final day in major championships in those palmy days, and as the afternoon wore on so the wind got stronger, blowing Hagen's chances away. Mehlhorn set the pace with a 78 for 301. Bobby Jones came to the last needing a birdie three to overtake him and got it. But Walker was still out on the course, gritting his teeth and punching the ball through the wind. He came to the last three daunting holes two shots ahead, needing three pars to win. And he did better than to get them; he even picked up a birdie, to win by three from one of the greatest golfers who ever played the game.

You can see how pleased Ernie was to see his fellow Englishman, whose career had followed such a similar pattern to his own, lift the trophy, by the slightly knowing but warm smile on his face as Cyril lifted the cup. As for Bobby Jones, he was, of course, graciousness personified. "Any man who can shoot the last nine holes in par today deserves to be champion," he told his constant companion and biographer, OB Keeler. "My hat's off to Cyril Walker."

Sadly this story of the unknown golfer who scooped one of the biggest prizes in golf does not have a happy ending. He blew his 1,000 dollar prize-money on unwise investments and drink and never won a significant tournament again, dying of poverty and pneumonia at the age of 56 in a Miami prison cell where he'd gone of his own accord, as he had nowhere else to live. Shades of Jackie Johnson.

After the excitements of the Open Ernie's life at Oakland Hills seems to have settled into a steady, comfortable routine. From what one can gather – given that most of Oakland Hills' records were destroyed in a disastrous clubhouse fire in 2022 – he was popular with the members,

(top) Ernie Foord, in white cap, presides at the presentation of the 1924 US Open trophy by Wynant D Vanderpool, USGA President, to Cyril Walker; (bottom) Cyril Walker receives the congratulation of runner-up Bobby Jones, the defending champion.

Following the destruction of the clubhouse by fire in February 2022, these grainy images are all that survive of Ernie Foord at Oakland Hills.

being treated, as with Hagen and Brady, as an equal rather than a servant, giving his lessons, managing his shop and playing as much golf on his own two splendid courses as he chose. Because he could still play a bit. In 1929 he went round the fearsome South course in 69, playing with his son Stan, who had a more than respectable 73.

We don't know why he decided to leave Oakland Hills in the autumn of 1929 to move to Flint Golf Club, some 60 miles to the north-west. But it does seem to have been his decision, as the report in the *Detroit Free Press* in February 1930 announcing the recruitment of Al Watrous as the Oakland Hills pro speaks of Ernie Ford having 'resigned' at the end of the previous season. But the move may well have had something to do with the politics of the motor industry. Just as Oakland Hills was very much the golfing headquarters of the Ford motor company in Detroit, so was Flint the preserve of the Buick, Chevrolet and ultimately General Motors HQ in Flint. It isn't hard to imagine Flint's founding father, the formidable J Dallas Dort, Club President, being prepared to put very good money into luring popular Ernie Ford away from Jo Mack and his fellow Ford directors at Oakland Hills. PG Wodehouse's stories of American millionaires fighting over English butlers come to mind.

At any rate Flint was almost as swish as Oakland Hills, even if it hadn't acquired the added gloss of hosting an Open Championship. The course had been laid out by none other than Willie Park, Open Champion at Prestwick in 1887 and Musselburgh in 1889, and ran alongside Thread Lake to the North-East of the city. At around 6,700 yards it was another stiff test and has hosted many big events in Michigan golf.

More than that, I'm afraid we don't really know, when it comes to Ernie Ford's closing years in Flint. Contacts with the club in search of information have drawn a blank, and the fact that the Flint clubhouse was burnt down in the 1950s hasn't helped. What a strange coincidence it is that the clubhouses of all three of the clubs where Ernie spent his last 19 years should have burned down. Pity the poor biographer!

However, we have no reason to doubt that Ernie's final position as a golf professional gave any less pleasure to himself and his members than all of his previous ones, from Burnham onwards, especially if he had indeed been lured to Flint by the prospect of much gold. He died in harness, of a heart attack, in October 1941 at the age of 58, doubtless much mourned not only by his members at Flint but much further afield. Nor was he long out-lived by his brother Fred, who had spent the 1930s as pro at another high profile Mid-West club, the Tam O'Shanter. This was another Hugh Alison design, originally a 'stag club' for men only but which was forced to re-group and admit women after the bank crash of 1933. Fred, who had suffered health problems throughout his time in the States, died in Detroit in 1945. We don't kmow what contributed to the brothers' early deaths but it wouldn't be surprising if smoking didn't play a part, just as it did in the case of Charles Whitcombe. Judging by the photographs which have survived of that era, most golf professionals smoked like chimneys.

Ada, however, lived on for many years, without ever re-marrying. She died in Detroit in 1985, well into her nineties. As for their son Stan, he enjoyed a long career as a professional without ever scaling the heights of his father and uncle.

9

In conclusion

So how do we assess Ernie Foord as a golfer and as a man? He was clearly highly talented – witness all those course records, his win over JH Taylor and his feats with brother Fred in the USA. He equally clearly failed to do himself justice in tournament golf. A best finish of 19th in 11 appearances in the Open Championship must have been a deeply disappointing return and he never got past the quarter final in the News of the World. The newspaper report of his first encounter with JH Taylor in 1901 speaks of him 'suffering greatly from nervousness, especially at the start'. Now, he was only 17 and he was playing a three-times Open Champion but, even so, I wonder if it wasn't his nerves that prevented Ernie Foord from producing his best golf on the really big occasions.

He seems to have been at his most comfortable when playing alongside friends and relations. His course record 63 at Burnham was achieved playing with a member, Mr JM Warren. Likewise his 73 with a putter. By 1913, when he beat Taylor over 36 holes, the pair of them would have been the best of friends, as opposed to master-craftsman and apprentice. In the US his course record at Mission Hills was achieved in the company of three members, in a fourball, and for his victories over Vardon and Ray, Duncan and Mitchell and Barnes and Hutchinson, he had the reassuring presence of brother Fred by his side.

The unofficial league table produced by Ainsworth Sports for golfers for the decade 1900-1910 has Ernie down at 208th in the world, just two places higher than his near contemporary, James Bradbeer. Yet, as an all-round golf professional, he must have been in the top 20, if not the top ten. The job that he secured at Oakland Hills was one of the most sought after, not just in American golf but in golf worldwide. Consider those who held the job immediately before and after Ernie: Walter Hagen, ten majors to his name, Mike Brady, twice beaten in a play-off for the US Open and, in 1930, Al Watrous, three times PGA seniors champion and runner-up to Bobby Jones in the epic Open Championship at Royal Lytham St Annes in 1926.

His skill as a club-maker and his abilities as a teacher and manager must have had a lot to do with the plum jobs that Ernie secured, but equally there must have been a lot more to it than that. I think it is fair to assume from the references to the Foord family in the Burnham committee minutes that they were an intelligent, spirited, occasionally bolshie lot, not to be pushed around. Walter Foord must have been a multi-talented man and a fast learner to have, successively, supervised the building of the first course, no doubt doing a lot of the hard work himself, taking over at short notice as professional, having only recently learned the game and then, as head green-keeper, seeing two major extensions to the course through to fruition, its reputation as a championship venue secured.

He and his wife Sarah, as steward, made themselves indispensable to the club, with the result that Walter always knew he was on safe ground in his run-ins with the committee. He did at least once over-step the mark, earning himself a reprimand and caution from the Secretary, Col Caulfield-Stoker, after a member had complained of his 'impertinence'. One can imagine the exchange:

Retired Indian army officer: "Didn't think much of the greens today, Foord. Sand all over the shop."

Walter Foord: "Oh, is that so? Well, if you think you could do a better job when there's half a gale blowing, I'll gladly loan you a broom and a wheelbarrow, <u>sir</u>."

But I'll bet that the reprimand was delivered with a knowing smile!

Ernie sounds to me like a chip off the old block. He can have lacked nothing in self-confidence, or maturity, first to have been offered the job of professional at the age of 16 and second to have accepted it. His shop seems to have gone from strength to strength, judging by the investment that the club was prepared to make in new premises, windows and cabinets, and if the committee at one stage complained at the cost of his lessons – 2/6 per hour – then the fact that he could charge so much shows the quality of his tuition.

He clearly had a head for business, as well. Despite being on only a modest retainer from the club, and coming from the humblest of backgrounds, he had saved enough money by the age of 27 to be able to move out of his tied accommodation and buy a smart new villa in the town for himself and Ada.

The move to the USA was a shrewd one. It meant that he avoided the possibility of conscription, and he knew full well that a golf boom was underway on the other side of the Atlantic and that there was good money to be made. Besides – and I'm sure this was a major factor in the decision – golf professionals were not looked down on, treated like servants, in the States as they still were in Britain. To the members he would be 'Ernie', not 'Foord', and he would be invited into the clubhouse for a drink after a round, and treated not just as an equal but with real respect.

By the time he moved from Oakland Hills to Flint in 1930 Ernie Ford, as he'd become, was a wealthy man. Not wealthy by the standards of today's top professionals maybe, but earning a king's ransom as compared with club professionals back in England. It was what he must have dreamed of when he'd set sail with Ada and little Stan back in 1916. What a shame it was that he died so young, at the age of just 58, before he could enjoy the fruits of his labours in retirement.

As to his character he was, as we have seen, clearly self-confident, well-organised and shrewd. In his younger days, from caddy-hood onwards, he was probably a bit of a lad, fond of a drink or two in the Berrow Inn after a good tip from a member. And if he wasn't a tall man, he was certainly handsome, judging by those photographs at Oakland Hills, no doubt a favourite with the local girls in Berrow, foremost amongst them Ada Gard, whom he married just a month or so before baby Stan arrived!

I like to think of him with a big smile on that broad face, offering a few well-chosen words of advice to Sammy Woods maybe, or congratulating a pupil who had finally hit one out of the middle, or putting the finishing touches to one of his beautifully crafted drivers, or shaking the hands of all and sundry as he basked in the glow of that 73 with just his putter.

My only sadness is that we don't know more about Ernie Foord. His son Stan had a son and a daughter, Sheila Amli, last heard of in Clayton, Missouri, but my efforts to get in touch with anyone from the family have – so far – come to naught. But if an Ernie Foord descendant should happen to read these words, be he or she in Britain or the USA, do please get in touch with Burnham and Berrow Golf Club. We would love to know more about our unsung hero of a golfing genius.

Burnham and Berrow clubhouse in 2023

Index

Akerman, William 18,84
Alison, Hugh 46,62,80,96-7,106
Archdale, Major 62,70,84,89-90
Armour, Tommy 102
Armstrong, Eliot 18
Armstrong, JS 46
Ball, Tom 58
Ballesteros, Severiano 22
Barne, GD 46
Barnes, Jim 9,96,100,102,107
Bradbeer, Bob 7,10,31-2,93,96
Bradbeer, Charles 31-2
Bradbeer, Edwin 31-2
Bradbeer, Ernest 31-2
Bradbeer, Francis 31-2
Bradbeer, Fred 7,10,31-2
Bradbeer, James 31-2,56,60,107
Bradbeer, Richard 10
Brady, Mike 98,100,105,107
Braid, James 21,35-6,49,54-9,68,90,95
Burrington, Gilbert 25
Caulfield-Stoker, Col 108
Cawsey, Harry 89
Clark, Tom 98
Colt, Harry 46,51,56,62,83,96-7
Cruikshank, Bobby 102-3
Darwin, Bernard 10,21,55,58,60,72,87-9
Darwin, Charles 21
Day, Arthur 31-2
Day, Ernie 31-2
Day, Joe 32
Diegel, Leo 97
Dort, Dallas 105
Drunkenbrod, FW 101-2
Duncan, George 96,107
Dye, Peter 96
Evans, Chick 102
Foord, Ada (née Gard) 69,84,92,94,101,106,109
Foord, Bill 16,18,25,84
Foord, Ernie 7,9-11,16,18,22,24-5,30-43,47-62,65-8,71-98,100-110
Foord, Fred 9-10,16,25,31-2,68-9,84,94-8,102,106-7
Foord, Jerry 102
Foord, Sarah 16,22,24,33,60,69-70,84,89-90,94,108
Foord, Stanley 69,84,102,105-6,109-10
Foord, Walter 7,16,18,22-5,32-4,46,53,59,62,5,69-70,84,90,108
Fowler, Herbert 44,46,55-6,62-3,83,90,94
Francis, Peregrine 12
Frost, Mitford 12
Fry, Sydney 7
Gibson, Charles 14,16,18,34,57,60,65
Grace, WG 30
Hagen, Walter 99-103,105,107
Haines, David 19,66-7,85
Ham, Edward 32
Ham, Jack 32
Hammond, Peregrine 12,14,80
Hawkins, Norval 99
Herd, Sandy 55,90
Hicks, Mrs 81
Hill, Tony 7
Hobhouse, Henry 71
Holt, Cecil 92
Holt, Tom 13-4,18,46,50,84,90,92
Holt, William 13-4
Hood, Arthur J 97
Hunt, GH 47
Hutchings, Charles 73
Hutchinson, Horace 18,34,36,49,82
Hutchinson, Jock 9,96,107
Jessop, Gilbert 30-1
Johnson, Jackie 30,32,103
Jolson, Al 100
Johnson, W 24
Jones, Bobby 98,102-4,108
Keeler, OB 103
Kennard, Adam 23
Kennard, Canon 13-6,18,23-4,32,34,46,82,84,99
Kennard, Edmond 13
Kennion, Alice 46
Kirkaldy, Andrew 23,58,90
Lagle, Maggie 10
Luscombe, Mrs 93
Lysaght, Jack 7
MacGregor, Gregor 29
Mack, Joe 99-101,105
MacKenzie, Alister 96
Mehlhorn, Bill 102-3
Mitchell, Abe 96,107
Morrison, Mr 59
Ogg, Willie 102
Ouimet, Francis 72,95
Palmer, JH 33,62
Park, Willie 105
Pope, John 31-2
Prideaux-Brune, Capt 46
Rawlings, G 93
Ray, Ted 9,60,68,72,89-90,95-6,107
Richards, Philip 11
Ross, Donald 94,96,99
Sarazen, Gene 98,102
Sherlock, John 58
Smith, Macdonald 102
Spinks, H 24
Taylor, JH 7,9-11,18-24,29,31-2,34-45,49,51-8,60-2,68,72,90-1,107
Thompson, Bertha 46
Thornton, CI 29
Tillinghurst, AW 96
Travers, Ben 7
Umph, Felix 100
Vanderpool, Winant 104
Vardon, Harry 9,21,36,44-5,54-5,59,61-2,68,72,89-90,95-6,107
Walker, Cyril 102-4
Warren, JM 47-8,51,107
Watrous, Al 105,108
Wheeler, Heneage 23,33,48,73-4,76-82,84,86
Whitcombe, Arthur 16,34
Whitcombe, Bessie 16,60,89
Whitcombe, Charles 10,31-2,106
Whitcombe, Ernest 10,31-2,59-60,68-9,93
Whitcombe, Reg 10,31-2
Wodehouse, PG 105
White, Jack 56-7,68
Woods, Sammy 7,25,27-31,109

Books by Anthony Gibson

West Country Treasury
A Compendium of Lore and Literature, People and Places
with Alan Gibson (1989)

A Celtic Odyssey
(2009)

Of Didcot and the Demon
The Cricketing Times of Alan Gibson
(2009)

With Magic in my Eyes
West Country Literary Landscapes
(2011)

Gentlemen, Gypsies and Jesters
The Wonderful World of Wandering Cricket
with Stephen Chalke (2013)

The Coloured Counties
Literary Landscapes of the Heart of England
(2017)

Somerset's Summer
(2019)

Also as co-writer:

From Wiveliscombe to Whitehall
A Farmer's Life
by Fred Elliott (2011)

Rosey
My Life in Somerset Cricket
by Brian Rose (2019)

God Speed The Plough
A Story of Unpredictable Endeavour
by Wesley Wyatt (2023)

For details of which of these books are available and how to order them, visit **www.anthonygibsonbooks.co.uk**